Ready to Help?

IMPROVING RESILIENCE OF INTEGRATION SYSTEMS FOR REFUGEES AND OTHER VULNERABLE MIGRANTS

This work is published under the responsibility of the Secretary-General of the OECD. The opinions expressed and arguments employed herein do not necessarily reflect the official views of OECD member countries.

This document, as well as any data and any map included herein, are without prejudice to the status of or sovereignty over any territory, to the delimitation of international frontiers and boundaries and to the name of any territory, city or area.

Please cite this publication as:
OECD (2019), *Ready to Help?: Improving Resilience of Integration Systems for Refugees and other Vulnerable Migrants*, OECD Publishing, Paris.
https://doi.org/10.1787/9789264311312-en

ISBN 978-92-64-31130-5 (print)
ISBN 978-92-64-31131-2 (pdf)

The statistical data for Israel are supplied by and under the responsibility of the relevant Israeli authorities. The use of such data by the OECD is without prejudice to the status of the Golan Heights, East Jerusalem and Israeli settlements in the West Bank under the terms of international law.

Photo credits: Cover © Arthimedes/Shutterstock.com.

Corrigenda to OECD publications may be found on line at: *www.oecd.org/publishing/corrigenda*.
© OECD 2019

You can copy, download or print OECD content for your own use, and you can include excerpts from OECD publications, databases and multimedia products in your own documents, presentations, blogs, websites and teaching materials, provided that suitable acknowledgement of OECD as source and copyright owner is given. All requests for public or commercial use and translation rights should be submitted to *rights@oecd.org*. Requests for permission to photocopy portions of this material for public or commercial use shall be addressed directly to the Copyright Clearance Center (CCC) at *info@copyright.com* or the Centre français d'exploitation du droit de copie (CFC) at *contact@cfcopies.com*.

Foreword

The integration of refugees and other vulnerable migrants in the host countries is essential to foster social cohesion and promote the economic benefits of migration. OECD countries were taken by surprise by the recent increase in inflows of humanitarian migrants. The refugee population in OECD countries tripled in just four years, between 2013 and 2017. But in addition to the recent upsurge in refugees, there have also been an increasing number of migrants admitted to OECD countries on other grounds; many of them face similar vulnerabilities and challenges in integrating in the host country. The humanitarian crisis raised many challenges to the host countries, but reception systems largely managed the strain of coping with sudden, large and unexpected inflows of people seeking protection. Record inflows, however, leave a legacy of increased demand for integration. Successful integration is as much a challenge as providing initial reception. Failure on this front would carry significant economic and social costs, constrain future policy-making and weaken trust in government.

The OECD has worked with member countries for decades to support effective management of migration and the integration of migrants, especially the most vulnerable, into the labour market and society of their host countries. To support OECD countries in improving integration policies, the Secretariat launched in 2017 a Horizontal Project on Ensuring Better Integration of Vulnerable Migrants. This report highlights the main elements of this work. In particular, the report is aimed at informing, sharing policy experiences and good practices, and helping governments promote the integration of refugees and other vulnerable migrants. Integration is not only about what happens in the OECD countries which have granted protection to these migrants; it also embraces support in developing transit and host countries as well as return and reintegration of migrants who do not have leave to remain and those who later choose to return when the situation improves in their home country.

Drawing on expertise and recent experience, the report addresses two main questions: *How can we be better prepared and enhance international co-operation in the context of protracted refugee crises? How can we foster the integration and reintegration of refugees and other vulnerable migrants?*

To answer these questions, this report brings together contributions from numerous OECD Directorates in 22 thematic chapters, each focused on a specific integration issue. The report identifies areas for improvement in the capacity of OECD member countries to co-ordinate and react faster and better.

A key lesson drawn in this report is that countries cannot act alone. Co-operation and sharing information and good practices is required at the international level. Domestically, governments need to work with a wide variety of stakeholders involved in the integration of migrants: civil society, the private sector, social partners, and government bodies at the sub-national level. Without a whole-of-society approach, it is difficult to achieve sustainable integration. The public should also be made aware of how governments intend to address integration challenges. A plan of action for integration should be in place, identifying partners and roles, and providing continuity.

Acknowledgements

Ready to Help: Improving Resilience of Integration Systems for Refugees and other Vulnerable Migrants was prepared as an integral part of the OECD Horizontal Project on Ensuring Better Integration of Vulnerable Migrants. The report was written under the overall supervision of the OECD Secretary General, Angel Gurría, and the OECD Chief of Staff and Sherpa, Gabriela Ramos.

The OECD Directorate for Employment, Labour and Social Affairs (ELS) led the writing and co-ordination of chapters of this report, under the senior leadership of Stefano Scarpetta (Director of ELS), Mark Pearson (Deputy Director of ELS) and Jean-Christophe Dumont (Head of the International Migration Division). Jonathan Chaloff and Gilles Spielvogel supervised the organisation of chapters and managed the project.

The report is based on contributions from different directorates: the Centre for Entrepreneurship, SMEs, Regions and Cities (CFE); the Development Centre (DEV); the Development Co-operation Directorate (DCD); the Directorate for Education and Skills (EDU); the Directorate for Employment, Labour and Social Affairs (ELS); the Economics Department (ECO); the Public Affairs and Communications Directorate (PAC); the Public Governance Directorate (GOV); and the Statistics and Data Directorate (SDD). OECD committees also reviewed and commented on an earlier draft version of this report.

The report would not have been possible without contributions from the following authors: Lisa Andersson Caroline Berchet, Francesca Borgonovi, Yves Breem, Lucie Cerna, Jonathan Chaloff, Claire Charbit, Eva Degler, Maria-Vincenza Desiderio, Emily Farchy, Kathleen Forichon, David Halabisky, Charlotte Levionnois, Thomas Liebig, Antonella Noya, Marco Mira D'Ercole, Anna Piccinni, Rachel Scott, Katherine Scrivens, Rhea Ravenna Sohst, Gilles Spielvogel, Cécile Thoreau, and Theodora Xenogiani.

Joanne Dundon, Veronique Gindrey, Liv Gudmundson, Phillipe Herve, Lucy Hulett, Kate Lancaster, and Anna Tarutina provided statistical, editing, logistical and publishing support. The report was edited by Randy Holden.

Table of contents

Foreword 3
Acknowledgements 5
Abbreviations and acronyms 10
Executive summary 11
Key findings 14
    Facts and figures 14
    Policies to improve co-ordination of initial and long-term response 14
    Employment 15
    Education 15
    Health 16
    Housing 16
    Specific factors of vulnerability 16
    Solutions in countries of first asylum and origin countries 17
    Improving preparedness 17

Introduction: Why should we care about integrating refugees and other vulnerable migrants? 19

Chapter 1. Recent trends regarding inflows of refugees and other vulnerable migrants 21
    What do we know about recent trends regarding refugees and other vulnerable migrants? 22
    What is the expected economic impact of the recent inflows of refugees and other vulnerable migrants? 24
    What has been the multilateral response to the recent surge in inflows of refugees and other vulnerable migrants? 27
    Note 29
    References 30

Chapter 2. Integration of refugees and other vulnerable migrants 31
    What do we know about the integration of refugees and other vulnerable migrants? 32
    What do we know about the well-being of refugees and other vulnerable migrants? 33
    What do we know about the skills of refugees and other vulnerable migrants? 35
    What is hindering the labour market integration of refugees and other vulnerable migrants? 39
    What do we know about integration into the school system of refugees and other vulnerable migrant group children? 41
    What are the challenges related to housing for refugees and other vulnerable migrants? 43
    What are the challenges related to the health of refugees and other vulnerable migrants? 45
    What challenges do unaccompanied minors face? 48
    What specific challenges do refugee women face? 51
    How do very low-skilled refugees and other vulnerable migrants fare in terms of integration? 53
    How can multilevel governance contribute to successful integration in host countries? 56
    Can entrepreneurship facilitate integration of refugees and other vulnerable migrants? 58

What can be done to engage employers to hire refugees and other vulnerable migrants? 61
How can the contribution of civil society be fully harnessed in integrating refugees and other
vulnerable migrants? 63
What is the impact of channels of entry on the integration of refugees and other vulnerable
migrants? 66
How can first asylum, transit and destination countries be supported in integrating refugees and
other vulnerable migrants in host communities? 68
What have we learned about reintegration in the home country of former refugees and other
vulnerable migrants? 71
References 75

Chapter 3. Anticipating, monitoring and reacting to inflows of refugees and other vulnerable migrants 83

Can early warning mechanisms help prevent a crisis in the face of future large-scale inflows? 84
What information needs to be improved to better monitor integration outcomes and inform
integration policy? 85
References 87

Chapter 4. Policy approaches for the integration of refugees and other vulnerable migrants 89

Smoothing the transition from reception to integration 90
Improving short- and longer-term employability and access to social services 90
Promoting economic and social acceptance 91
Supporting sub-national authorities 92
Increasing international co-operation on crisis management and integration 92
References 94

Tables

Table 2.1. Checklist of public action for migrant integration at the local level 56
Table 2.2. Progressing towards comprehensive solutions for local integration 71

Figures

Figure 1.1. New asylum applications since 1980 in the OECD area and the European Union 22
Figure 1.2. Relative change in the labour force due to increased inflows of asylum seekers between
 2014 and 2017 in Europe 26
Figure 2.1. Employment rate by immigrant categories and duration of stay, European OECD
 countries, 2014 32
Figure 2.2. Selected well-being outcomes for migrants and the native-born population 33
Figure 2.3. Distribution of education among Syrians and Afghans in selected transit or destination
 countries 36
Figure 2.4. Education level of refugees in the Zaatari camp in Jordan, by gender 38
Figure 2.5. Overview of risk and protective factors for the well-being of immigrant children 41
Figure 2.6. Key practices to favour integration of family migrants: Lessons from ntegration reviews
 in OECD countries 53
Figure 2.7. Adults with very low literacy proficiency (Level 1 or below), by country of birth 55
Figure 2.8. Self-employment rates of immigrants and natives by country, 2015 59
Figure 2.9. Number of third country nationals ordered to leave, persons returned, and the return rate
 (%) in the European Union, 2008-16 73

Boxes

Box 1.1. Recent emigration from Venezuela and demands for international protection 23
Box 1.2. The labour market impact of Syrian refugees in Turkey, 2011 to the present 27
Box 2.1. Piloting skills assessment in refugee camps 38
Box 2.2. Migrants' right to health 47
Box 2.3. Unaccompanied minors in schools 50
Box 2.4. Integrating refugee women who arrive in the context of family migration 53
Box 2.5. Widespread low literacy proficiency among migrants 55
Box 2.6. Financing integration at the local level 58
Box 2.7. !gnite, Australia 60
Box 2.8. The OECD-UNHCR Action Plan for Engaging with Employers in the Hiring of Refugees . 61
Box 2.9. The social impact bond – A new model for funding integration? 65
Box 2.10. The Japanese resettlement programme 66
Box 2.11. Agricultural partnership programme for resettled refugees in the United States 68
Box 2.12. The Jordan Compact 69
Box 3.1. Big data use in early warning systems to detect risk of forced migration 84
Box 3.2. The International Forum on Migration Statistics 86

Follow OECD Publications on:

 http://twitter.com/OECD_Pubs

 http://www.facebook.com/OECDPublications

 http://www.linkedin.com/groups/OECD-Publications-4645871

 http://www.youtube.com/oecdilibrary

 http://www.oecd.org/oecddirect/

Abbreviations and acronyms

ACAF	Association of Self-Funded Communities (Associació de Comunitats Autofinançades), Spain
AFAD	Disaster and Emergency Management Agency (Afet ve Acil Durum Yönetimi Başkanlığı), Turkey
AMIF	Asylum, Migration and Integration Fund, European Union
AVRR	Assisted Voluntary Return and Reintegration
BAMF	Federal Office for Migration and Refugees (Bundesamt für Migration und Flüchtlinge), Germany
CRRF	Comprehensive Refugee Response Framework
DAC	Development Assistance Committee, OECD
DiPAS	Displaced Persons in Austria Survey
EASO	European Asylum Support Office
EMN	European Migration Network
EU LFS	European Union Labour Force Survey
EU SILC	European Union Statistics on Income and Living Conditions
EWCS	European Working Conditions Survey
GCR	Global Compact on Refugees
ICMC	International Catholic Migration Commission
IDPs	Internally displaced persons
IOM	International Organization for Migration
IP	Part of the longer abbreviation TCP/IP, Transmission Control Protocol/Internet Protocol
ISCED	International Standard Classification of Education
JRC	Joint Research Centre, European Union
NSOs	National statistical offices
ODA	Overseas development aid
ORR	Office of Refugee Resettlement, United States
PIAAC	Programme for the International Assessment of Adult Competencies
PISA	Programme for International Student Assessment, OECD
RAPP	Refugee Agricultural Partnership Program, United States
RHQ	Refugee Assistance Headquarters, Japan
SNIS	Swiss Network for International Studies
UN DESA	United Nations Department of Economic and Social Affairs
UN OCHA	United Nations Office for the Coordination of Humanitarian Affairs
UNHCR	United Nations High Commissioner for Refugees
UNICEF	United Nations International Children's Emergency Fund
VET	Vocational education and training
WHO	World Health Organization

Executive summary

Most of the six million refugees in OECD countries arrived in the last five years as part of the largest inflows in recent history. The challenges faced by OECD countries in ensuring the integration of refugees and other vulnerable migrants have been heightened by this increase in inflows of migrants seeking protection. There are lessons to be learned from these recent inflows for other crisis situations, elsewhere or in the future. In many regions around the world, humanitarian crises may induce large migration flows, especially in developing countries. Risk factors that may trigger other humanitarian crises are not likely to diminish in the future. The international community must address the integration needs of the most vulnerable, including people affected by forced displacement, but also other migrants in situations of vulnerability.

Record inflows, which have abated in some countries but which continue in others, have left a legacy of increased demand for integration into the labour market, education system and society. The integration of refugees and other vulnerable migrants is a crucial objective. By improving the employability of refugees and other vulnerable migrants, countries can help them realise their full economic potential and generate a positive economic impact. This also improves their acceptance and social inclusion in the local community. Failure to integrate refugees and other vulnerable migrants not only increases social exclusion and tension but would sharply constrain policy options in addressing future inflows.

This report aims to support OECD countries to be better prepared to ensure integration of refugees and other vulnerable migrants, notably in the context of sudden and large inflows. Building on the recommendations of the Global Compact on Refugees as well as on previous OECD work, and drawing on the recent experience of OECD countries, this report identifies a number of policies that can improve integration and support origin and transit countries.

The first lesson drawn from this analysis is that, contrary to frequent public perception, the systems in place in OECD countries have largely proven capable of coping with sudden, unexpected inflows of people seeking protection. Countries have, in most cases, successfully provided emergency reception and addressed the immediate needs of vulnerable migrants. Most mainstream education and employment services continued to function adequately. However, this is not to ignore the cases where services have not kept up with unprecedented demand, or where standards of service have been compromised; these are situations which provide important lessons for better preparing for the strain of future sudden arrivals.

The resilience of systems in the face of the challenge was largely due to ad hoc measures, rather than to pre-established rapid response plans. Government flexibility in responding should be seen positively, but came at a high cost. Channels of consultation and collaboration with partners within each country and abroad had to be newly established. In addition to higher financial costs, the lack of a plan created a public perception of uncontrolled migration flows and a breakdown of systems. The political crisis which ensued was larger than the humanitarian situation would have justified.

The second lesson is that ensuring integration of refugees and other vulnerable migrants is a long-term commitment more challenging than initial reception. Evidence from OECD countries shows that while refugees and other vulnerable migrants understandably lag behind other migrants in terms of labour market integration, a wide range of policies have proved effective for their integration in the medium and long-term.

A third lesson is that no country can address the complexity of integration of refugees and other vulnerable migrants alone. Host countries can share the burden of response to spikes in demand for international protection, can help each other to be better prepared and informed, and can share good practices. Integration in one host country may have spillovers on the perception and prospects of vulnerable migrants in other countries. Failures in one country may complicate policy development in others.

Another area for international co-ordination is in promoting greater coherence between humanitarian, development, and peace actors in their support to developing host countries, where 85% of the world's refugees are located. Stronger partnerships in targeting aid and assistance can help achieve mutual objectives for integration and protection of refugees and other vulnerable migrants. Development co-operation and other types of financial assistance for situations of forced displacement can also ease pressure on these countries. Another form of burden sharing with developing host countries is to provide resettlement and complementary legal pathways for people in need of protection.

Similarly, a fourth lesson is that no central government can ensure integration without working with other actors. The UN Global Compact on Refugees recognises the role of relevant stakeholders, including local authorities, civil society and the private sector, among others. Similarly, the UN Global Compact for Safe, Orderly and Regular Migration calls for national integration policies to include local authorities and, as appropriate, civil society organisations, employers' and workers' organisations and other stakeholders, such as third sector organisations and social enterprises. Sub-national levels of government such as local authorities have a role to play and need to be involved. A whole of society approach is necessary, sharing responsibilities according to appropriate multi-level governance arrangements.

A fifth lesson is that continuity of public action is key for an effective response. Many OECD countries have boosted budgets for supporting the integration of refugees and other vulnerable migrants. Those resources are adequate as long as an effective plan is in place. Such a plan must take a whole-of-society approach, involve multiple stakeholders and levels of government, identify different target groups and partners, and establish robust evaluation and feedback mechanisms. There are several elements to continuity. First, the plan must be consistently supported over time. Institutional capacity and knowledge should be preserved even when interventions wind down. Second, vulnerable migrants must be supported with different interventions along their journey from origin to host country and through all phases of settlement and integration. Return to origin countries when warranted and support for voluntary return and reintegration is an integral part of continuity.

OECD countries can be better prepared for future large inflows of refugees and other vulnerable migrants. In part, this requires improved early warning systems, but also the development of channels of collaboration with partners – internationally and domestically

– which can be quickly activated. Communication with the public is part of the response. Better information about the integration of refugees and other vulnerable migrants helps establish appropriate policies, helps migrants choose the best-suited activities to achieve their own integration, and shape realistic expectations in the public. There is an ample toolkit of specific policy interventions which support integration of refugees and other vulnerable migrants. As many OECD countries emerge from a crisis phase, it is important that feedback from recent experience be included in rapid response plans for the future. There is no reason to be caught off-guard or unequipped.

Key findings

Facts and figures

OECD countries have seen record inflows of asylum seekers and refugees in recent years. From mid-2013 to mid-2017, the refugee population in OECD countries has tripled, from 2 million to 5.9 million. European countries received 4 million asylum applications between January 2014 and December 2017, three times as many as during the previous four-year period.

In relative terms, for European countries as a whole the impact of the recent refugee inflow is estimated to be small. By December 2020, refugees will have increased the working-age population by no more than 1/3 of one percent, according to projections.

Refugees have much poorer labour market outcomes than other migrants or the native-born. In the past, they've taken as much as two decades to catch up with the native-born in terms of employment. The average employment rate of refugees in the first five years after arrival, in Europe, is only one in four.

More than half of refugees arrive with low education levels. Skills tests also show a large share with low skill levels. In addition to refugees, other migrants are more likely than natives, in most countries, to have low skill levels, which make them vulnerable to being excluded. Moreover, those with tertiary education face considerable hurdles in having their skills rewarded in the labour market of the host country.

The cost of integrating refugees varies significantly across OECD countries, estimated between 0.1 and 1% of GDP, but should be seen as an investment in their success and in their future contribution to the economy of the host country. One element of these costs are the in-donor refugee costs counted by OECD DAC countries as overseas development aid (ODA), which increased sharply from 4.2 billion in 2013 to 16 billion in 2016.

Policies to improve co-ordination of initial and long-term response

Most OECD countries were caught off guard by recent increases in demand for protection by displaced populations. The early warning systems in place were inadequate or poorly integrated into the policy making process, leaving signals unread. Better preparation of OECD countries for future crises requires improvement in early warning systems, but also their interaction with relevant authorities, in particular at the local level. Even in the absence of explicit warnings, scenario building can help guide policy choices when crises emerge.

At the international level, the crisis saw a remarkable effort to achieve co-ordination. However, co-ordination on managing movements and sharing information is still uneven between destination, transit countries and countries of first-asylum. The crisis also revealed the risk that failures in integration in one country could have spillover effects in other countries. Co-ordination on integration has taken on a new importance.

Migrants tend to be concentrated in urban areas and integration performance differs according to place of residence. Recent experience has shown the importance of involving local, sub-national and national governments. Within countries, multi-level governance is important to ensure that actors are in contact and collaborate with each other. The continuity and sustainability of integration measures has been less a product of funding than of collaboration with many actors and the assurance of public support.

The statistical infrastructure for monitoring flows and integration outcomes is still inadequate in many countries to capture essential information on the characteristics of migrants and their outcomes over time. Policy evaluation and development of responses requires more information than currently available. Steps should be taken to fill gaps.

Employment

Delaying labour market access has in some countries prevented refugees from starting their integration process. Accelerated recognition of refugee status and labour market access, especially for asylum seekers who are likely to be granted protection, has helped speed up their integration. Legal, transparent, simple and rapid pathways to access the labour market should be in place for recognised refugees. This includes access to mainstream employment support services, and procedures to assess and recognise skills acquired abroad, as well as personalised counselling services. Skills assessment should produce profiles which can be used to inform both migrants and their potential employers.

Lack of language proficiency is a major barrier, and language support – especially occupation-specific support – should be one of the first integration measures. Language courses should be adapted to the profile of beneficiaries and employment prospects.

Employers have a key role to play in facilitating the integration of refugees and other vulnerable migrants, but have been largely left out of policy response in many countries. Governments can increase employer interest in hiring refugees by providing legal certainty, and support after hiring.

Newcomers unfamiliar with the labour market – including refugees and other vulnerable migrants - face the risk of exploitation. Countries should enforce equal treatment with nationals and other migrants in terms of working conditions, wages, and access to redress for violations.

Entrepreneurship is one way for migrants to integrate in the labour market, but is especially challenging for refugees due to language barriers, lack of prior experience, and difficulty in accessing credit. Coaching and community-based finance can help entrepreneurship be a solution for some refugees.

Education

School integration for refugee children is more complex than for other migrant children. Refugee children often need more time to adjust to the new education system, and may have additional vulnerabilities related to trauma experienced in their home country and during their journey, and from extended periods without schooling.

Vocational education needs to be adapted for refugees and other vulnerable migrants. Information and orientation are essential to help choose the right pathway, while bridging education, including language education, may be necessary to prepare for mainstream programmes. Pathways to higher education should also be considered.

Health

Health systems need to cope with and adapt to an increase in the number of refugee patients with multiple and complex physical and mental health needs. In addition to experience with violence in their home country, many refugees experienced trauma during flight and even reception, complicating their health situation.

Better coordination between healthcare providers is needed to improve the efficiency in service delivery. Triage should be improved to ensure that those with specific health needs are directed to places where appropriate care is provided.

Housing

Finding adequate reception facilities and longer-term housing solutions for refugees has been difficult in a context of shrinking access to low-cost housing and constraints on supply, in particular in urban areas.

Dispersal, one of the main policy responses to inflows of large numbers of refugees, is meant to limit segregation and congestion of services in areas where demand is concentrated. However, dispersal may also prevent the creation of a critical mass of users for support services and keep refugees far from areas rich in job opportunities. Co-ordination with local governments is necessary to improve buy-in – including by rural areas and those with declining populations – and identify the profiles best suited for integration in each context. Poorly matched placements, and unprepared, underfunded or unengaged local partners, can lead to excessive secondary movements and undo the benefits of dispersal policy.

Specific factors of vulnerability

Among refugee and vulnerable migrants, a number of factors contribute to additional vulnerability and require specific responses. Unaccompanied minors in particular face additional risk of mental health problems, exploitation by criminal networks and difficulty in integrating in school. Policies to address their needs are resource-intensive, requiring trained support. Rapid provision of a guardian and school enrolment are important, as is guidance in managing the transition to adulthood and the end of special support.

Another target group where employment outcomes have been poor and slow to improve is refugee women, who are at higher risk of trauma during flight. There is a high return of language proficiency and education for refugee women on the labour market and on the education and employment prospects of their children, especially their daughters. Yet enrolment of women with children into standard language courses has been difficult, due to cumulating factors, including conflict with childcare commitments. More flexible arrangements can increase participation in training.

Low-skill and low-educated migrants fare poorly, and low-educated refugees even worse. Very low language skills can potentially be addressed through workplace training, especially as low-educated migrants have employment levels which are at least as high as those of low-educated natives.

Resettled refugees are selected from among the most vulnerable of all refugees in countries of first asylum. Resettlement, however, opens the possibility for pre-arrival preparation and training and intensive post-arrival case management and support. This is important because resettled refugees often have serious health problems, low education, and other vulnerability factors, and are more likely than other refugees to comprise families and women.

Private sponsorship is one way through which refugees can benefit from personalised integration services, beyond what governments can provide on an individual basis.

Solutions in countries of first asylum and origin countries

Integrating forcibly displaced people into host communities in developing countries is fraught with challenges, some of which could be overcome with greater coherence between humanitarian, development and peace actors. Achieving coherence requires several key elements: a common risk-informed content analysis to define a collective outcome; the mobilisation of aid instruments according to their comparative advantage to meet the objective; and political leadership to overcome institutional barriers and strategically review partnerships. Regional plans can also improve coherence.

In terms of reducing pressure in developing host countries, resettlement is an important contribution. For less vulnerable refugees –generally excluded from resettlement channels – complementary pathways for study or work can provide an attractive alternative to remaining in the developing host country.

Return to origin countries, always challenging, is becoming more important. The recent increase in people seeking protection meant an increase in the number of rejected asylum seekers, requiring return. Their sustainable return and reintegration is facilitated by work at the community level in countries of origin. Voluntary return, of migrants who wish to go back when the situation in their home country improves, also implies co-operation with the country of origin. Policies should engage migrants in the process, plan return at the community level and provide post-return support. Efforts to ensure transfer of skills and the ability to use acquired skills can bring benefits to the origin country as well as the person returning.

Improving preparedness

Countries should develop a crisis response plan in advance, identifying partners, channels of communication and responsibilities in the face of large inflows of people seeking protection.

Early warning systems can contribute to prepare public authorities for imminent likely spikes in demand for protection or other inflows of vulnerable migrants. Such systems were in place in many countries but were insufficiently connected with response mechanisms. New data sources offer unprecedented opportunities for monitoring risk, and should be explored. Such systems require a high degree of collaboration and take time to develop.

Following major shocks and crises, a "post-mortem" exercise should be conducted by authorities to improve data and channels of communication, and ensure that signals are transmitted and acted upon.

Since no country can address the challenges alone, international co-operation should start with developing a response plan and extend to implementation. Channels need to be in place for concertation and distributing responsibility and roles, as well as sharing effective practices. The Global Compact for Safe, Orderly and Regular Migration offers a framework for strengthening co-operation.

Regarding preparedness in developing host countries, donors and partners should work together for crisis prevention.

Authorities have struggled in recent years to communicate basic facts about refugees and about policy response. The response plan should include a framework for working with the media and providing the public with clear information about the strategy and initiatives planned and undertaken and about the results achieved. This can reduce the risk that shocks, even when successfully managed, lead to political crises.

Introduction: Why should we care about integrating refugees and other vulnerable migrants?

Global refugee stocks are now at their highest levels in history – the latest figures indicate that about six million refugees now live in OECD countries. Most of them arrived in the past five years as part of record recent inflows of refugees in OECD countries, especially in 2014-16.

While total flows have diminished in the last two years, there are lessons to be learned from these recent inflows for other crisis situations, elsewhere or in the future. Indeed, today there are many regions around the world where humanitarian crises induce large migration flows, especially in developing and emerging countries. Whereas OECD countries may learn from these situations, the experience of integration policies implemented by member countries also constitutes a collective knowledge that may be useful in other countries. Risk factors that may trigger other humanitarian crises are in fact not likely to diminish in the future, including in the vicinity of many OECD countries. One way to be better prepared to deal with these future risks is to conduct a comprehensive assessment of the country-level and multilateral responses to the refugee inflows of the past five years.

Integrating refugees and other vulnerable migrants (see) for a definition of this group) is an objective of utmost importance, for two reasons. First, by improving the employability of refugees and other vulnerable migrants, host countries can help them realise their full economic potential and thus benefit from the positive economic impact. Secondly, improving employability improves the acceptance and social inclusion of refugees and other vulnerable migrants in the local community. Failing to integrate these people carries costs – in terms of social exclusion, tension and more unequal societies. Moreover, it could sharply constrain policy options to address future inflows.

This report builds on a collective OECD effort that has mobilised resources and expertise across the organisation and involved the endeavours of diverse committees and working parties. It gathers evidence on many dimensions of the integration process of refugees and other vulnerable migrants in origin, transit and destination countries, in terms of both economic and social outcomes and the policies in place to respond to the challenges posed by the arrival of larger-than-usual inflows.

The report focuses on how to improve the resilience of systems. This includes the immediate coping capacities in the event of external and unplanned shocks; the ability to absorb the shock in the short-term emergency; adaptive capacities in order to recover from the consequences of these shocks and to mitigate losses; and transformative capacities in the long term in order to anticipate similar crises and alleviate their consequences.

The first part of this report provides an overview of the recent flows of migrants seeking protection, discusses the expected economic impact of these flows, and presents the milestones of the multilateral response. The second part discusses the many dimensions of integrating refugees and other vulnerable migrants, in terms of their economic and social outcomes as well as specific factors of vulnerability. It also provides a comprehensive assessment of the policies put in place to support the livelihood and integration of refugees and other vulnerable migrants in destination and transit countries, as well as in origin countries upon return. The third section of the report tackles issues of anticipation, monitoring and reacting, examining the role of early warning mechanisms and the challenge of improving information to better monitor integration outcomes and frame policies.

This report tries to respond to the challenges posed by the unexpected arrival of relatively large inflows of refugees and other vulnerable migrants, taking account of the complexity involved in hosting and integrating people who have not chosen to leave their home. Although finding solutions to these issues is by no means simple, the experience accumulated by OECD countries in this area provides knowledge that will help avoid past mistakes and improve the efficiency of the response in similar situations in the future.

Who are refugees and other vulnerable migrants?

In this report the word "refugees" is used as a generic term to include all beneficiaries of international protection – both those who obtained formal refugee status and those who received other forms of protection, notably subsidiary protection. The term "vulnerable migrants" refers to those who have characteristics and face integration challenges similar to refugees but who have been admitted on other grounds and have a legal right to stay. When reference is made to survey data, these generally relate to persons who self-declare having migrated for purposes of international protection. The report considers asylum seekers, who are candidates for international protection status, separately from refugees.

Chapter 1. Recent trends regarding inflows of refugees and other vulnerable migrants

In recent years, OECD countries have witnessed large inflows of refugees and other vulnerable migrants. This chapter reviews the evidence on the magnitude of these inflows and their expected economic impact, and discusses the multilateral response which has been brought about.

What do we know about recent trends regarding refugees and other vulnerable migrants?

The world's refugee population has increased significantly in recent years, from 11.1 million in mid-2013 to 19.9 million in mid-2018. During this period, the refugee population in OECD countries has nearly tripled, from 2 million to 5.9 million, while it has more than doubled in the European Union (from 920 000 to 2.1 million). This is due in part to the massive displacement occasioned by the Syrian War. However, conflicts and humanitarian crises in other countries have also played a role (e.g. in Afghanistan, Iraq, Sudan, the Horn of Africa and Central America). Despite the rapid increase in the number of refugees hosted by OECD countries, this still represents a relatively small fraction of the 28.5 million people forcibly displaced outside their home countries worldwide.

New asylum applications reached a record level in the OECD area and the European Union in 2015 and 2016 (Figure 1.1). European countries received 4 million asylum applications between January 2014 and December 2017, three times as many as during the previous four-year period. About one-quarter (960 000) of those applications were made by Syrian nationals. During the same period (2014-17), about 1.6 million individuals were granted some form of protection in European countries, including 780 000 Syrians (OECD, 2018[1]).

Figure 1.1. New asylum applications since 1980 in the OECD area and the European Union

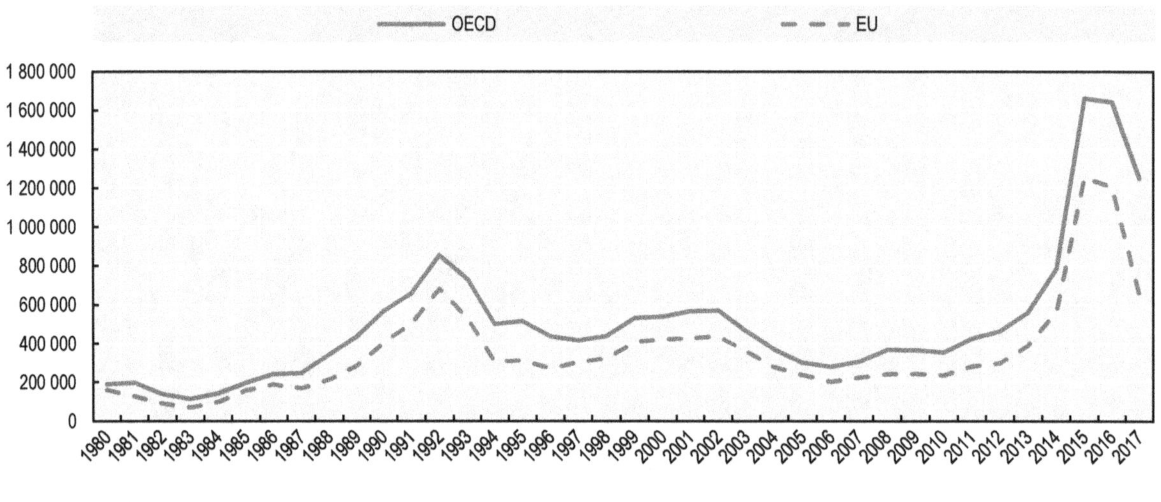

Note: Preliminary data for 2017.
Source: UNHCR, Eurostat.

Although the inflow numbers of migrants seeking protection in European countries in the past three years have been high by historical standards, they have remained much lower, in both absolute and relative terms, than inflows experienced by countries neighbouring Syria. In November 2018, about 3.6 million Syrians benefited from temporary protection in Turkey, 1 million in Lebanon, and about 670 000 in Jordan. Turkey has been the leading destination country for refugees in the OECD area for seven years, and is the top refugee-hosting country in the world.

Other OECD countries have witnessed increasing inflows of humanitarian migrants. In Canada for example, permanent entries for humanitarian reasons have increased from an average of 25 000 per year in 2011-14 to 32 000 in 2015 and to almost 60 000 in 2016. In 2017, permanent entries for humanitarian reasons declined by 30%, due to the decrease in the number of resettled refugees brought to Canada.

Along with other Latin American countries, Mexico, Chile and Colombia have also witnessed a recent increase in asylum applications from Venezuelans due to the deteriorating economic and political situation in that country (see Box 1.1). Spain and the United States have also witnessed increased asylum applications from Venezuelan nationals.

For European countries, the decline in asylum applications that began in the second half of 2016 has continued in 2017 and 2018, with 50 000 to 60 000 monthly applications compared to 130 000 between July 2015 and September 2016. Despite this slowdown, because of the time required to process asylum claims, the number of pending applications remains very high at 880 000 in August 2018, including those from almost 100 000 Syrians.

The sharp increase in asylum seeker inflows in 2015 and 2016 compared to previous years had little effect on the age and gender distribution of asylum applicants or accepted refugees in European countries. Throughout the period 2011-17, about 71% of asylum applicants were aged 18-64, whereas children (aged 0-17) represented about 29%. In addition, three-quarters of working-age asylum applicants were men. These characteristics of asylum applicants do not differ significantly from those of accepted refugees. By contrast, the share of children among Syrian refugees in Turkey is significantly higher (40%), while the share of men among working-age refugees is smaller (56%).

Box 1.1. Recent emigration from Venezuela and demands for international protection

In the past few years, the complex socio-economic and political situation in the Bolivarian Republic of Venezuela has caused many Venezuelans to move to neighbouring countries and beyond. More than 3 million now live abroad, most of whom left in the past three years. Their primary destinations were Brazil, Colombia, Costa Rica, Mexico, Peru, Spain and the United States. According to figures provided by host governments, about 360 000 Venezuelans lodged new asylum claims since the beginning of 2015, including more than 200 000 in 2018. More than 40% of asylum applications were made in Peru, 20% in the United States, 18% in Brazil and 8% in Spain. In addition, by October 2018 almost 1 million Venezuelans had accessed alternative legal forms of stay under national or regional frameworks, including in Colombia (415 000), Chile (130 000), Peru (110 000), Ecuador (97 000) and Argentina (93 000). However, the majority find themselves in irregular situations. Without access to some form of legal status, they are at a higher risk of violence, exploitation, sexual abuse, trafficking, and discrimination. While the responses of states were generous, host communities receiving Venezuelans were also under increasing strain as they sought to extend assistance and services to those arriving.

Source: OECD/ILO/IOM/UNHCR (2018[2]).

There are groups of migrants in vulnerable situations apart from persons seeking international protection. The number of unaccompanied migrant children, for example, has increased sharply in recent years in the United States and in many European OECD countries. Between 2014 and 2016, European OECD countries received more than 180 000 asylum applications from unaccompanied minors, and the United States reported almost 170 000 border apprehensions of unaccompanied minors. While some of these unaccompanied children are also applicants for international protection, all of them are in situations of vulnerability and require special consideration and case management by host countries.

Another group of migrants in a situation of vulnerability are those with very low levels of education. This group includes many who have sought international protection, but also migrants who have legal status and arrived through other channels. Among immigrants who arrived in OECD countries in the past five years, at least 4.4 million had less than secondary level education, including some with little or no formal education at all.

What is the expected economic impact of the recent inflows of refugees and other vulnerable migrants?

Recent inflows of refugees have a sizeable potential economic impact – both due to the fiscal cost of hosting a larger-than-usual number of asylum seekers and refugees, and in terms of labour market adjustment since a large share of new refugees are of working age. This also includes the cost of processing a large number of asylum applications and, more importantly, providing subsistence to asylum seekers while their applications are being examined.

Frequently, before gainful employment is obtained, a significant proportion of refugees will continue to be dependent on the welfare systems of host countries. For numerous refugees, access to the labour market and proper social integration are conditional on adequate language training, as well as professional training if necessary; both are often largely financed by public funds. Although such expenses can strain local and national budgets in the short run, they can also have a positive impact on the economy by boosting aggregate demand. An OECD analysis (OECD, 2017[3]) focusing on countries having recently received a relatively high number of asylum applications as a share of the population has shown that fiscal costs peaked in 2016 in most of these countries, ranging from 0.1% to 1% of GDP.

The additional labour force provided by refugees has in some cases also been considered a potential means to alleviate labour shortages in the context of an ageing European workforce. The recent refugee inflows, however, occurred as many European countries were recovering from the deep global financial crisis and were still facing high levels of unemployment. In that light, the public's perception has not always been positive; there have been fears of detrimental effects on wages or employment, especially for low-skilled native workers.

Historical evidence suggests that large inflows of migrants seeking protection in OECD countries have generally had little impact on the labour market outcomes of the native-born at the national level. Some studies have even noted that the skill complementarity between refugees and natives can have positive consequences for natives. Other works have noted more significant negative effects at the local level or for specific population sub-groups – for example, when refugees compete for the same jobs as the native-born. This is the case in Turkey, the country hosting the largest number of refugees worldwide. Due to constraints in obtaining work permits, most Syrian refuges have found employment in the informal sector, which has led to significant employment losses for the native-born in that sector.

For European countries as a whole, the estimated relative impact of recent refugee inflows on the size of the working-age population is small, projected to reach no more than one-third of 1% by December 2020 (OECD, 2018[1]). In terms of labour force, since participation rates of refugees are typically very low in the early period of their stay in the host country, the magnitude of the aggregate net impact is estimated to be even smaller, at less than one-quarter of 1% by December 2020. For about half of European countries, refugee arrivals will have virtually no impact on the labour force, and most other European countries will experience only a moderate impact by the end of 2020. The impact is expected to be significantly higher in Austria, Greece and Sweden, however, with at least a 0.5% increase in the labour force and up to 0.8% in Germany (Figure 1.2). In countries with the highest aggregate effects, the impact is again likely to be much stronger in specific segments of the labour market: among young low-educated men in Austria and Germany, it could reach about 15%.

Turkey alone is currently hosting more than twice as many Syrians as the total number of Syrians who have received some level of protection in all EU countries since January 2014. As from November 2018, about 3.6 million Syrians benefit from temporary protection in Turkey. Among these, about 240 000 reside in refugee camps administered by the Turkish Government; most of the camps are located near the Syrian border. Outside the camps, Syrian refugees now make up nearly 10% of the population of several border cities. The largest metropolitan areas, especially Istanbul and Ankara, as well as the Aegean coast also attract many refugees seeking job opportunities (OECD, 2018[1]).

Figure 1.2. Relative change in the labour force due to increased inflows of asylum seekers between 2014 and 2017 in Europe

Cumulative change estimated in December 2017 and December 2020

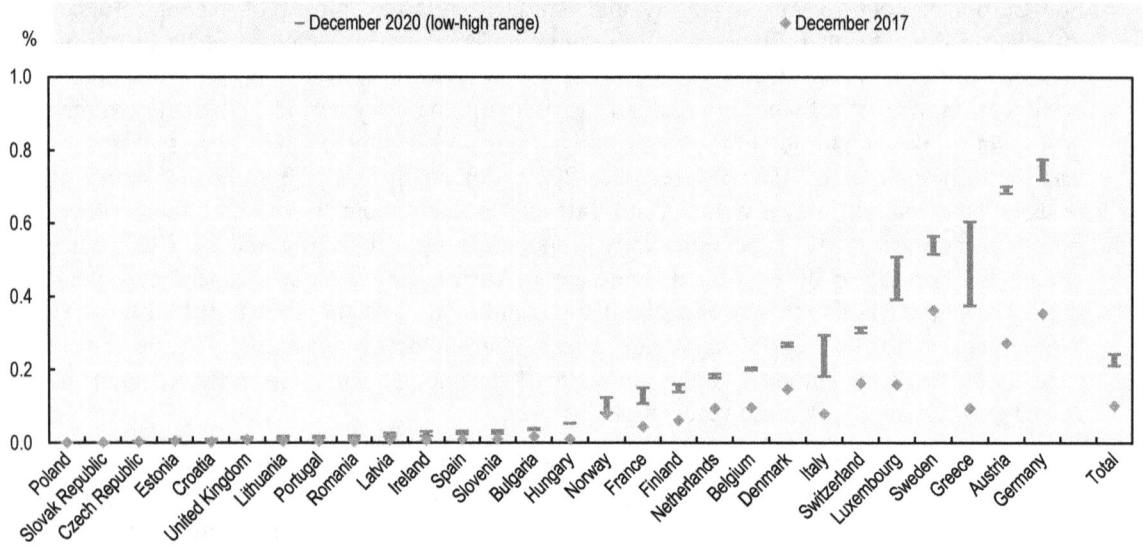

Notes: Includes EU-28 countries, Norway and Switzerland. The relative change in labour force is the difference between the estimated refugee labour force accounting for increased inflows since January 2014 and the counterfactual refugee labour force (i.e. assuming that asylum applications in 2014-20 remain equal to the 2011-13 average), divided by the total labour force in December 2013. Up to December 2017, observed data on asylum applications and decisions are used; for 2018-20, it is assumed that asylum applications are either equal to the 2011-13 average or to the 2017 average, generating the December 2020 low-high range.
Source: Eurostat: asylum statistics, labour force statistics; OECD estimates.

Access to the labour market is a key issue for Syrian refugees, with many taking up informal jobs. Prior to January 2016, refugees could only apply for a work permit if they held a residence permit, which was the case only for a small minority. Under the current regulation, Syrian refugees can apply for a work permit six months after being registered under temporary protection. These permits, however, are only valid in the locality of registration, which limits their attractiveness: most Syrian refugees are registered in border areas with few employment opportunities. Securing a formal job in another location therefore requires registering for and obtaining a work permit in that location. As a result of these constraints, less than 14 000 work permits had been issued to Syrians at the end of 2016. Although there was an increase in 2017 with about 21 000 permits delivered, and although Syrians involved in seasonal work in agriculture are still exempted from requiring a work permit, these figures remain well below the number of Syrian refugees in need of work (see Box 1.2).

> **Box 1.2. The labour market impact of Syrian refugees in Turkey, 2011 to the present**
>
> As of November 2018, the 1.9 million working-age Syrian refugees living in Turkey represented about 3% of the total working-age population of the country, with a much higher proportion in border cities as well as in Istanbul and Ankara. Due to the constraints in obtaining work permits, it is estimated that most Syrian refugees in employment have informal jobs, which are common in Turkey (about 20% of total employment).
>
> Several recent papers have attempted to estimate the impact of Syrian refugees on the Turkish economy, and particularly on the labour market. Ceritoglu et al. (2017[4]) find that immigration has negatively affected the employment outcomes of natives in the south-eastern border area, while its impact on wages has been negligible. They document notable employment losses among informal workers as a consequence of refugee inflows, although formal employment increased slightly, potentially due to increased demand for social services. They also find that disadvantaged groups (women, younger workers and less-educated workers) have been affected to a greater extent, and that the prevalence of informal employment in the Turkish labour market has amplified the negative impact of Syrian refugee inflows on natives' labour market outcomes. Del Carpio and Wagner (2016[5]) find similar results: Syrian refugees induce large-scale displacement of the native-born in the informal sector. There are also increases in formal employment for the Turks – though only for men who have not completed high school education. The less educated and women experience net displacement from the labour market and, together with those in the informal sector, declining earning opportunities.

What has been the multilateral response to the recent surge in inflows of refugees and other vulnerable migrants?

The recent surge in refugees led to an unprecedented multilateral response, with the question of integration appearing on the international policy agenda as never before.

A World Humanitarian Summit[1] was held in Istanbul in May 2016, organised by the UN OCHA on the basis of the Agenda for Humanity published by the UN Secretary-General. Among other objectives, the Summit aimed at initiating a set of concrete actions and commitments to enable countries, local governments and communities to better prepare for and respond to crises, and to withstand shocks. Integration of refugees and other vulnerable migrants was one issue area where a number of states and non-state actors made commitments. The OECD has committed to support member countries in their efforts to strengthen integration programmes for refugees; to make development co-operation more efficient, effective, innovative, and focused on building resilience in situations of forced displacement; and to improve consistency, comparability and transparency in the reporting of in-donor refugee costs, so as to enhance accountability and contribute to the quality and effectiveness of aid.

At the European Union level, a multilateral and concerted response by Member States took a number of different forms. Support was arranged for countries exposed to sudden large inflows. The EU also co-ordinated Member State actions on integration. For example, in June 2016 it adopted an Action Plan on the Integration of Third-Country Nationals, which provides a comprehensive framework to support Member States' efforts in developing and strengthening their integration policies, alongside measures taken by the European Commission. The Action Plan targets all third-country nationals in the EU, and includes actions to address the challenges faced by refugees. It also redefines the approach for EU funding for integration. The EU directs that funding through its 2014-20 Asylum, Migration and Integration Fund (AMIF), which exceeds EUR 3 billion and covers actions that include those favouring integration of third-country nationals. In 2017, the Commission also established a "European Partnership for Integration" with social and economic partners at European level, to work more closely together to promote a faster and more effective integration of refugees in the European labour market. In addition, there is increased support to local and regional authorities, in particular through the Urban Agenda Partnership on the Inclusion of Migrants and Refugees.

At the OECD, the Development Assistance Committee (DAC) has developed new guidelines on reporting in-donor refugee costs. These reveal a steep increase in costs among DAC members, especially in Europe. Prior to 2013, in-donor costs were about USD 2 billion annually in EU countries, with a similar amount in non-EU countries. In 2016, they reached USD 12.3 billion, before falling slightly in 2017 to USD 11.2 billion. In non-EU members, they hit 3.6 billion in 2016, before falling to 2.5 billion in 2017. While overseas development aid (ODA) helped support costs of the immediate response to this crisis, many observers argued that these are not in line with the main ODA objective of promoting the economic development and welfare of developing countries. In 2017, new clarifications to the reporting directives on in-donor refugee costs were agreed upon, which will improve the consistency, comparability, and transparency of DAC members' reporting of these costs.

The most important event in multilateral response was the high-level plenary meeting on addressing large movements of refugees and migrants held at the United Nations in September 2016. The New York Declaration for Refugees and Migrants (UN General Assembly, 2016[6]), which followed the meeting, addressed for the first time at this high level the need for a comprehensive response.

For both refugees and migrants, the Declaration by the General Assembly committed to "measures to improve their integration and inclusion, as appropriate, and with particular reference to access to education, health care, justice and language training". The document also called for national policies to be developed "as appropriate, in conjunction with relevant civil society organizations, including faith-based organizations, the private sector, employers' and workers' organizations and other stakeholders". The Declaration further encouraged governments and civil society to interact more deeply, in light of the role of civil society in promoting "the well-being of migrants and their integration into societies, especially at times of extremely vulnerable conditions".

A further outcome of the 2016 event was the commitment to a Global Compact on Refugees (GCR). The Compact aims to facilitate access to durable solutions, which include "the three traditional durable solutions of voluntary repatriation, resettlement and local integration, as well as other local solutions and complementary pathways for admission to third countries, which may provide additional opportunities". The final draft was released in July 2018, with a plan to develop indicators and a timeline to increase the number of resettlement places.

As part of the GCR, the General Assembly committed to implementing a Comprehensive Refugee Response Framework (CRRF), covering reception and admission; support for immediate and ongoing needs; support for host countries and communities; and development of durable solutions. In this framework, the OECD and UNHCR have developed a monitoring system of the use of complementary pathways for admission of those with international protection needs. The OECD has also been working on "funding and effective and efficient use of resources". This input is to come through a survey of trends in ODA from DAC members to programmes and projects focused on refugee-hosting, as well as future funding plans and other efforts.

Integration appeared more prominently in the work of the G20. Among the policy priorities to which the ministers committed in their statement at the G20 Labour and Employment Ministers Meeting in May 2017 was "Promoting the fair and effective integration of regular migrants, recognised refugees and returning migrants in labour markets, in accordance with national law" (G20 Labour and Employment Ministers, 2017[7]). The statement's Annex also contains a number of points targeting integration of refugees and other vulnerable migrants.

Note

[1] www.agendaforhumanity.org/summit.

References

Ceritoglu, E. et al. (2017), "The impact of Syrian refugees on natives' labor market outcomes in Turkey: Evidence from a quasi-experimental design", *IZA Journal of Labor Policy*, Vol. 6, http://dx.doi.org/10.1186/s40173-017-0082-4. [4]

Del Carpio, X. and M. Wagner (2016), "The impact of Syrians refugees on the Turkish labor market". [5]

G20 Labour and Employment Ministers (2017), *Ministerial Declaration: Towards an Inclusive Future: Shaping the World of Work*, Bundesministerium für Arbeit und Soziales, Bad Neuenahr, http://www.bmas.de/SharedDocs/Downloads/DE/PDF-Pressemitteilungen/2017/g20-ministerial-declaration.pdf?__blob=publicationFile&v=2 (accessed on 09 September 2018). [7]

OECD (2018), *International Migration Outlook 2018*, OECD Publishing, Paris, http://dx.doi.org/10.1787/migr_outlook-2018-en. [1]

OECD (2017), *OECD Economic Outlook, Volume 2017 Issue 1*, OECD Publishing, Paris, http://dx.doi.org/10.1787/eco_outlook-v2017-1-en. [3]

OECD/ILO/IOM/UNHCR (2018), *G20 International Migration and Displacement Trends Report 2018*, http://www.oecd.org/els/mig/G20-international-migration-and-displacement-trends-report-2018.pdf (accessed on 12 December 2018). [2]

UN General Assembly (2016), *New York Declaration for Refugees and Migrants: resolution / adopted by the General Assembly,*, https://refugeesmigrants.un.org/declaration (accessed on 09 September 2018). [6]

Chapter 2. Integration of refugees and other vulnerable migrants

Indicators of integration of refugees and other vulnerable migrants reveal outcomes which are worse than other categories of migrants. This chapter reviews the evidence on outcomes for refugees and other vulnerable migrants, identifies factors of vulnerability and obstacles to their integration, and reviews actors, actions and strategies which can favour their integration.

What do we know about the integration of refugees and other vulnerable migrants?

Refugees represent one of the most vulnerable groups of migrants on the labour market. In European countries, their employment rate is 56%, just three percentage points higher than for family migrants, but nine percentage points lower than for native-born persons (EU/OECD, 2016[1]).

On average, it takes refugees up to 20 years to attain an employment rate similar to that of the native-born (Figure 2.1). Five years after arrival, only one in four refugees is employed, the lowest of all migrant groups.

Figure 2.1. Employment rate by immigrant categories and duration of stay, European OECD countries, 2014

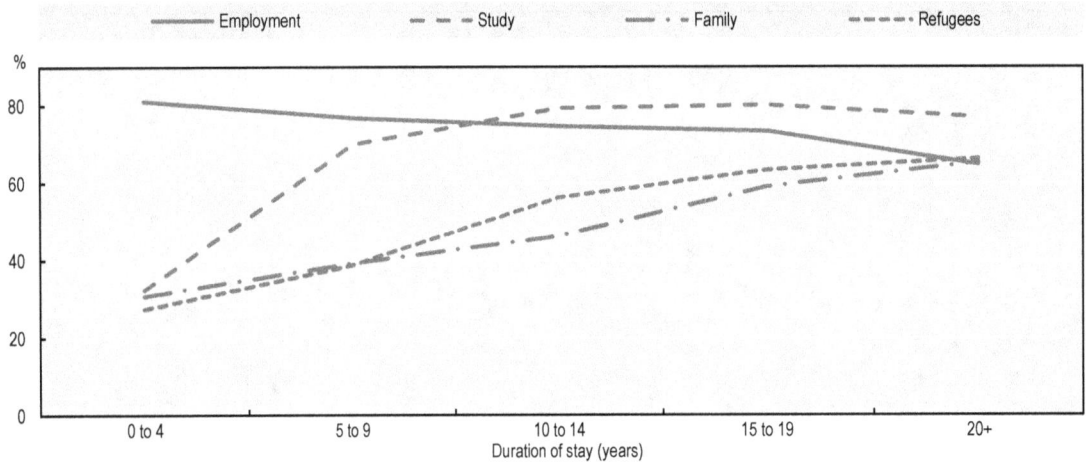

Source: EU/OECD (2016[1]).

A significant part of the difference in the employment rates between refugees and other migrants is explained by differences in education level – refugees are more often found among the less educated, whose employment rate is far below average.

Bringing refugee women into employment is a particular challenge. Their employment rate is on average 45%, 17 percentage points lower than that of refugee men and 6 percentage points lower than that of other women not born in the EU.

This result is to some extent driven by the fact that nearly half of refugee women have a low level of education, a substantially higher share than that for other migrant groups. It also reflects the low activity rates of refugee women relative to men, 57% versus 77%.

Knowledge of the host country language has a considerable impact on the employment outcomes of refugees, which holds across education levels.

Refugees are much more likely to be overqualified than other migrants. In total, almost 60% of employed tertiary-educated refugees in the EU are overqualified for the jobs they occupy, more than twice the level of the native-born and also well above the levels for other migrant groups.

The observed widespread discounting of refugees' formal qualifications relates to the fact that most of them have foreign qualifications that employers have difficulties in evaluating; also, refugees often lack documentation of their degrees.

What do we know about the well-being of refugees and other vulnerable migrants?

Relatively poor outcomes in terms of labour market integration translate into lower well-being for migrants in general, and notably so for the most vulnerable ones. In a majority of OECD countries, migrants have a worse situation than the native-born population on almost all well-being outcomes (Figure 2.2). In terms of household income, housing conditions, life satisfaction, social support and students' skills,[1] migrants in at least 75% of OECD countries experience worse outcomes than the native-born population. Trust in the political system is the only indicator where migrants report better outcomes than the native-born for a majority of OECD countries.

Figure 2.2. Selected well-being outcomes for migrants and the native-born population

Share of all OECD countries, %

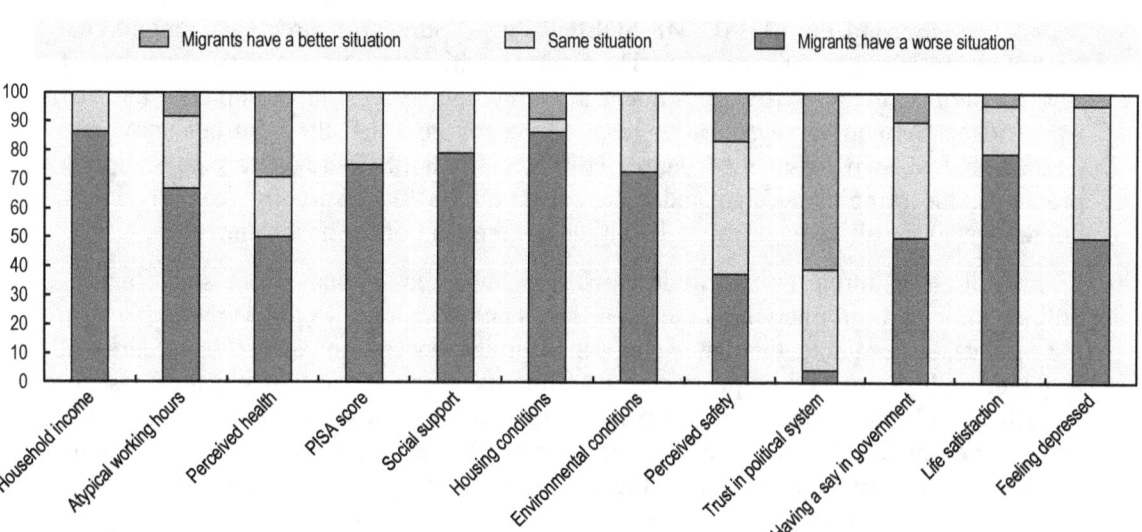

Source: OECD (2017[2])

One area where differences between migrants and the native-born are particularly stark is job quality. Migrants are more likely to work in low-paid jobs and are twice as likely to experience in-work poverty compared to natives. In OECD countries, on average, 20% of foreign-born employed people has income below the poverty threshold conventionally used in OECD studies (half of equivalised median income) in 2015, compared with 10% of the native-born (OECD/EU, 2018[3]). Migrants are also more likely to be overqualified for their jobs: 35% of migrants with a tertiary degree perform a job that requires a lower level of qualification, compared with 31% of the native-born (OECD/EU, 2018[3]).

Migrants also face greater exposure to risky or harmful working conditions. Across countries covered by the European Working Conditions Survey (EWCS), migrants report riskier employment conditions than do the native-born population. According to the survey, in Sweden, France and Spain more than half of all migrant employees are employed in jobs that involve one or more risks to their physical health.

Moving from one country to start life again in another is a defining event that presents migrants with an entirely new context for every aspect of their lives. While this move can open up people's opportunities to achieve better lives, it can also expose migrants to challenges and hardships that they would not otherwise have experienced – including living far away from friends, family and all the things that make a place feel like home.

At the same time it is also clear that some migrants are more vulnerable than others. In particular, refugees and asylum seekers are likely to have substantially lower well-being outcomes than other types of migrants when first arriving in the host country, as forced migration entails higher costs and risks than other forms of migration (Brücker, 2016[4]). Unfortunately, these are the people who are least likely to be represented in conventional household surveys.

Recognising that people who have undergone forced migration are likely to have very different needs and experiences, some countries have implemented specially targeted surveys to capture their well-being outcomes. Examples include the "Building a New Life in Australia" survey, a five-year longitudinal study conducted between 2013 and 2018 by the Australian Institute of Family Studies with support from the country's Department of Social Services; and the IAB-BAMF-SOEP Refugee Survey, a three-year longitudinal study launched in Germany in 2016. These surveys have to contend with a number of specific hurdles, including translation and interpretation issues. For example, in the first wave of the German survey, 90% of respondents reported that they did not know any German before arriving in the country (Brücker, 2016[4]). There were also sampling problems: the sampling design and data collection for such surveys generally cover migrants who are officially registered with the government of the host country.

Overcoming the hurdles is worth it, however, since the findings from such surveys provide important information on the experiences and outcomes for this vulnerable group of migrants. For example, the first wave of the German survey showed that one-quarter of respondents had survived shipwrecks; two-fifths had been victims of physical assault; one-fifth had been robbed; more than half had fallen victim to fraud; more than one-quarter had been blackmailed; and 15% of female refugees reported having been sexually assaulted. The Australian survey also highlighted the widespread experience of traumatic events, showing a far greater prevalence of moderate-to-high levels of psychological distress among survey participants than among the general population. For example, 35% of male and 45% of female respondents were at moderate or high risk of psychological distress in the four weeks prior to the survey, compared with 7% of men and 14% of women in the general population (Jenkinson et al., 2016[5]). Nonetheless, respondents to the Australian survey also indicated that they were settling in well in their new country, with 84% of them saying that their overall experience had been good or very good; they cited feelings of safety and the fact that their children were happy as the main factors helping them in their new lives (Jenkinson et al., 2016[5]).

What do we know about the skills of refugees and other vulnerable migrants?

The integration of refugees is generally more difficult than the integration of other immigrants, for a variety of reasons related as much to their socio-demographic profile as to the conditions under which migration occurred. For those who have a solid educational background, it is important to assess the skills they possess, and to identify obstacles to the use of their skills.

Information on the educational attainment of recent refugees is relatively scant and arises from disparate sources, at different stages of the asylum process. As a result, there are no comprehensive and comparable data across OECD countries.

However, even refugees with low educational attainment do not arrive without skills. In addition to cognitive skills and experience, refugees bring their hope and dedication to rebuilding of their life. They indeed have strong motivation, which can be harnessed with appropriate policies.

Assessment of refugees' skills is difficult, however. In some countries surveys have provided assessment of educational attainment for asylum seekers, while in others this information is available only for refugees. Figure 2.3 shows the distribution of education among Syrian and Afghan refugees (two of the main origin countries of recent refugee inflows) in various OECD transit or destination countries. Overall, their educational attainment is relatively low, although the share of post-secondary educated is markedly higher among Syrian refugees. There are also differences across migration stages and refugee categories: the share of those who are tertiary-educated is much lower among Syrian refugees in Turkey than among Syrians who arrived in Sweden or in Austria. In Canada, Syrian refugees who benefited from private sponsorship were much more likely to have post-secondary education than those resettled under government sponsorship.

While international analyses are limited, there are some promising studies and initiatives. For example, the OECD in collaboration with the World Bank undertook a pilot study to assess the skills of the refugee population with the OECD tool Education & Skills Online (Box 2.1).

At the national level, some countries have utilised tools and carried out surveys to assess the skills of refugees. In Germany for example, the IAB-BAMF-SOEP-Refugee Survey gathered information on newly arriving asylum seekers and refugees between 2013 and January 2016. The survey collected responses on the educational level, qualifications and knowledge of German language of respondents, and also tested their cognitive skills through a math test. Results indicate that refugees with higher ISCED levels (4 and above) scored higher on the math test than those with lower ISCED levels. Analyses indicate that this test is a suitable indicator for assessing cognitive potential and a complement for estimating the skills potential of refugees, ultimately contributing to successful integration (Brücker, Rother and Schupp, 2017[6]).

Figure 2.3. Distribution of education among Syrians and Afghans in selected transit or destination countries

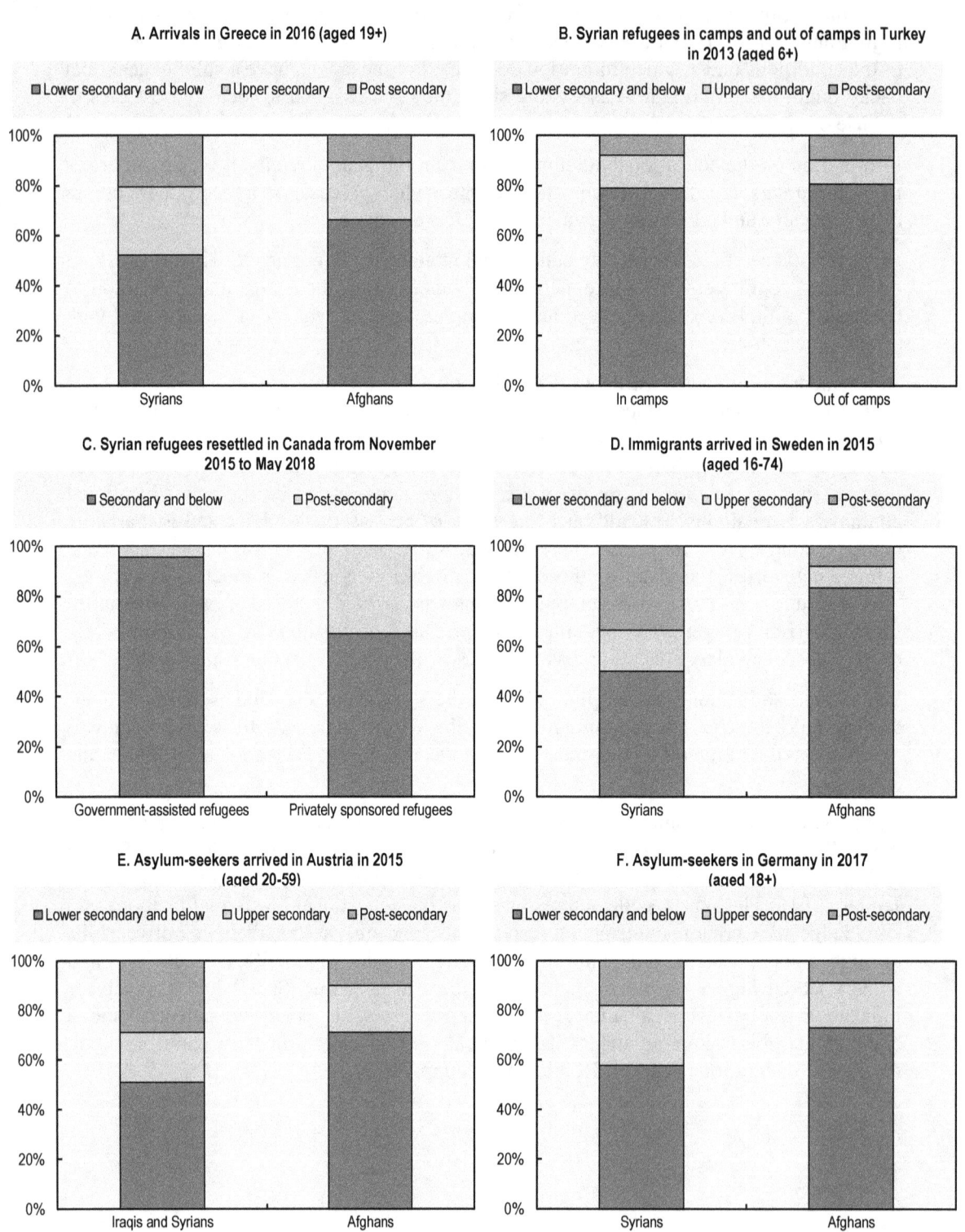

Source: Panel A – UNHCR (2016); Panel B – Turkish Disaster and Emergency Management Agency (AFAD) (2013); Panel C – Immigration, Refugees and Citizenship Canada; Panel D – Statistics Sweden; Panel E – Displaced Persons in Austria Survey (DiPAS); Panel F – German Federal Office for Migration and Refugees (BAMF) (2018).

Matching the aspirations and skills of migrants to vocational pathways is a challenge. Many recently arrived migrants are unfamiliar with the vocational education and training (VET) system, the occupations it covers, its labour market outcomes and outcomes of alternative pathways. Some may arrive with a negative view of vocational pathways. For others, financial constraints mean that they cannot afford to earn only apprentice wages during the initial training period, even though future returns would make it a worthwhile investment. Finally, some people may also have insufficient skills – notably language skills – to enter VET, and need support and preparation.

Some may benefit from acquiring basic technical skills, learning about the cultural codes of the workplace, or expanding their occupation-specific vocabulary. Finding an apprentice position in a company can also be a challenge, so migrants could benefit from support with writing applications and preparing for interviews. Once young people enter VET, many struggle to cope with the academic workload, especially when they also have weaknesses in language skills. Most integration programmes provide language courses prior to VET, but students who have not acquired sufficient language proficiency may struggle in vocational schools that do not provide additional language support.

While some employers facing skills shortages are particularly keen to hire apprentices, many struggle to work with those who have limited language proficiency. A recent survey of German employers found that support with occupation-specific language was the most important measure that could help them offer more apprenticeships to refugees (OECD, 2017[7]). Cultural differences are also a challenge, as some apprentices may struggle to adapt to a new working culture (e.g. arriving on time).

Financial and personal challenges can also affect the rates at which refugees complete apprenticeship programmes. Dropping out is sometimes caused by financial hardship – for some, an apprentice wage to invest in a better future is simply not affordable. Personal difficulties (e.g. fear of deportation, concerns about family members left behind) also make completion difficult.

> **Box 2.1. Piloting skills assessment in refugee camps**
>
> Education & Skills Online is an assessment tool designed to provide individual-level results that are linked to the OECD Survey of Adult Skills (PIAAC) measures of literacy, numeracy and problem solving in technology-rich environments. In addition, the assessment contains non-cognitive measures of skill use, career interest, health and well-being. It was piloted in 2017 in refugee centres and camps in Greece and Italy, in four languages (English, French, Arabic and Farsi). Respondents were asylum seekers 18 years of age and older from the main arrival countries. Sampling was designed to be representative of the adult population staying at reception centres. There were 2 446 respondents in Italy (12% women), from Nigeria, Gambia, Senegal, Eritrea, Mali, Côte d'Ivoire, Guinea, Somalia and Sudan. In Greece, 1 681 individuals were surveyed (34% women) from Syria, Afghanistan and Iraq. Findings reveal low skill and minimal literacy levels among the surveyed individuals. Results differed according to origin country; respondents in Greece performed better than those in Italy (World Bank, 2018[8]).
>
> Similar analyses have been done in refugee camps in developing countries. As part of a matching and employment initiative, the Jordan Compact (see Box 2.12), a skills mapping questionnaire, was organised in the Zaatari camp in Jordan. The survey covered previous experience, educational level, previous training, knowledge of national laws and regulations relating to work, and technical/functional skills in the manufacturing, garment and other sectors, as well as incentives that would induce them to accept a job. Most survey participants had completed ninth grade; women on average had a higher level of education than men (Figure 2.4). The study further showed that a majority of both men (75%) and women (54%) were willing to take up a job outside the camp, and interested in and willing to gain new skills in order to find employment.
>
> **Figure 2.4. Education level of refugees in the Zaatari camp in Jordan, by gender** 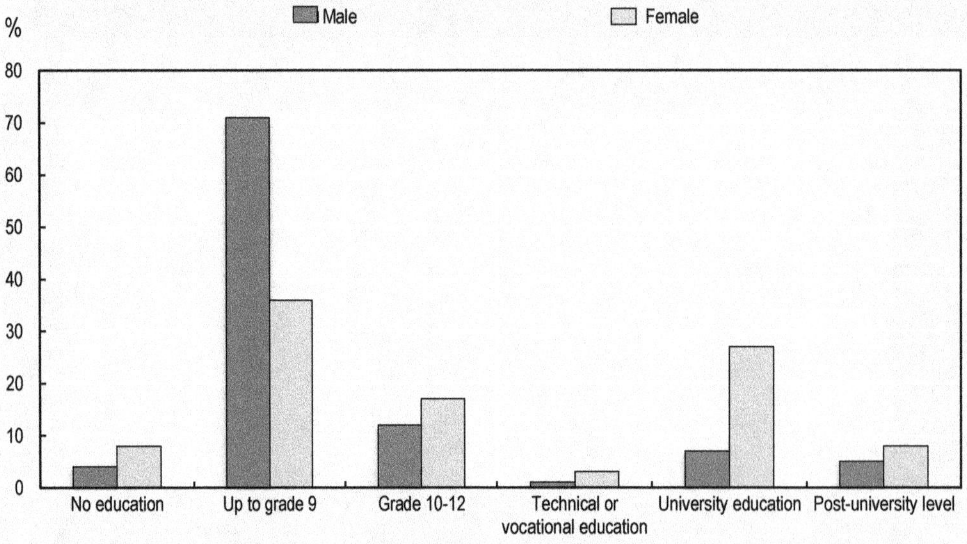
>
> *Source*: (UNHCR, 2017[9]).

What is hindering the labour market integration of refugees and other vulnerable migrants?

The active participation of all immigrants – including the most vulnerable – in the labour market as well as in society is crucial for ensuring social cohesion in the host country and migrants' ability to function as autonomous and productive citizens. Integration is a mutual, dynamic and multifaceted process. From the perspective of the migrant, integration requires both the capacity to understand and the willingness to adapt to the lifestyle of the host society without having to lose one's own cultural identity. From the perspective of the host society, it requires the willingness and the capacity to be welcoming and responsive to migrants' needs.

Along the integration process, several obstacles can hold refugees and other vulnerable migrant groups back from integration. Although many of them apply in varying degrees to all newly arrived immigrants, refugees have four specific factors of vulnerability:

- First, they have, on average, lower educational attainment than the native-born and other migrants.

- Second, they are more likely to have suffered trauma.

- Third, as they have not chosen to migrate, they generally have had no opportunity to prepare for their life in the new country.

- Fourth, refugees often arrive in the context of large-scale inflows, which means they compete with each other for employment.

As a result, refugees do not start from the same position on the labour market and in the host society as other migrants. Data for the European OECD countries show that – after controlling for other relevant individual characteristics – refugees have employment rates that are 23 percentage points lower than their peers who have come as labour migrants (EU/OECD, 2016[1]).

Mastery of the host country language is crucial to succeed in local labour markets and to utilise previously acquired qualifications. It is also a precondition for participating in society at large. It brings greater social contacts with native speakers and higher likelihood of pursuing higher education opportunities and moving across the country. Refugees had little or no time to learn the host country language prior to arriving, and may have low education levels that hinder language acquisition.

Less than half (45%) of refugees in the EU reported having an advanced knowledge of the host-country language, compared with two thirds of other migrants from non-EU countries. There is a strong negative correlation between language difficulties and labour market outcomes, notwithstanding entry categories or the level and country of qualification. If refugees had the same command of the host-country language as natives, their employment rates would be 10 percentage points higher than their actual levels, whereas the gains would be lower for all other migrant groups (EU/OECD, 2016[1]).

However, depending on the national legislation, not all vulnerable groups have access to publicly funded language training; in many OECD countries, asylum seekers and those under temporary protection do not.

More broadly speaking, vulnerability arises from the lack of skills that are transferable and valued in the host country. In 2012-13, an average of a little over one in four immigrants of working age, or 25 million, were poorly educated.

Evaluation of immigrants' skills is strongly determined by their mastery in the host country language. Overall, according to the 2012 PIAAC survey, immigrants have markedly lower levels of literacy (in the host country language) than people born in the host country. Gaps are widest among the poorly educated, particularly in Sweden, Norway, France, the Netherlands, Austria, and Germany. Across the OECD area and the European Union, around two in five foreign-language immigrants (who did not learn the host country language in their childhood) have no more than basic literacy skills (at best equivalent to PIAAC Level 2); among these, more than a half have inadequate literacy skills (at best equivalent to PIAAC Level 1).

Foreign-born individuals whose mother tongue is different from the language of the test tend to have lower literacy and numeracy proficiency and poorer labour market outcomes than individuals whose mother tongue matches the language of the test. However, the size of the language penalty varies considerably, both among and within countries, as it is related to the degree of proximity between the mother tongue spoken by migrants and the language in which the respondent did the test. The penalty is particularly pronounced for those migrants who arrived in the host country after the age of 12, and persists irrespective of length of stay (OECD, 2018[10]).

Highly educated refugees and other vulnerable migrants trained abroad face difficulties in having their qualifications recognised and valued on host country labour markets. These markets tend to devalue foreign qualifications, which affects employment, leads to overqualification and reduces wages (Bonfanti and Xenogiani, 2014[11]). Employment returns to education abroad – as measured by the increase in the probability of being in employment with an additional year of education – are only a little more than half the returns of domestic qualifications, both in Europe and the United States.

The downgrading of foreign qualifications in host country labour markets holds even after controlling for differences in years of residence and literacy skills (OECD, 2014[12]). It is a key issue in integration, since two-thirds of immigrants hold foreign degrees (OECD/EU, 2015[13]). Estimates suggest that between one-third and one-half of the high level of overqualification of immigrants compared with the native-born is associated with lower skills at given qualification levels (Bonfanti and Xenogiani, 2014[11]; OECD, 2007[14]). However, it is unclear to what extent the undervaluing of foreign qualifications may be ascribed to the poor performance of education systems in countries of origin, or to the limited transferability of skills.

Host country employers downgrade foreign work experience even more than they do foreign qualifications. However, evidence (Picot and Sweetman, 2011[15]) suggests that attitudes change once immigrants become more familiar with the local labour market and employers have information that enables them to better judge the value of foreign qualifications and work experience.

Some refugees and other vulnerable migrants must overcome trauma before they can enter the labour market. Some arrive with health issues because of exposure to unfavourable environments and lack of access to medical facilities, or physical violence or trauma requiring specific attention and adequate medical and psychological support.

Another element of refugees' vulnerability, related to unpreparedness, is a lack of networks or understanding of labour markets, which affects their ability to seek jobs and access recruitment channels, even when their qualifications are at least comparable to those of their native-born peers. They are at an obvious disadvantage when it comes to knowledge of the host country's labour market and hiring practices, and with respect to contacts, direct or indirect, with employers.

The lack of direct contact between employers and immigrants also fuels the former's misgivings about the latter's skills and productivity. A Swedish study (Åslund, Hensvik and Skans, 2014[16]) found that managers are generally much more likely to hire workers with the same ethnic background they have.

Networks are part of the broader issue of knowledge of a local labour market and how it functions. Writing applications and presentation in a job interview tend to be highly country-specific. Differences in this respect are wide, even among OECD countries.

Discrimination on the grounds of race, ethnicity or nationality is also a factor that hinders the access of immigrants, notably to the job and housing markets. In the OECD and EU areas, between 2002 and 2012, one immigrant in seven felt that they were discriminated against on the grounds of their origin. Perceived discrimination is more widespread among men and people born in lower-income countries. Situation and CV-testing studies have demonstrated discrimination in hiring in many OECD countries (OECD, 2014[12]). Immigrants and their offspring have to regularly send out more than twice as many applications before they secure a job interview.

What do we know about integration into the school system of refugees and other vulnerable migrant group children?

The integration of refugee children and other vulnerable groups (such as unaccompanied minors – discussed below – and asylum-seekers) in school systems is important for their academic outcomes, as well as for their social and emotional well-being. The success (or lack of) integration in schools can also affect the future labour market integration potential of these children. The risk and protective factors for the well-being of immigrant children in school (Figure 2.5) apply to refugee children as well. However, research is still sparse on what policies and practices work for integrating refugee children and the children of other vulnerable migrants.

Figure 2.5. Overview of risk and protective factors for the well-being of immigrant children

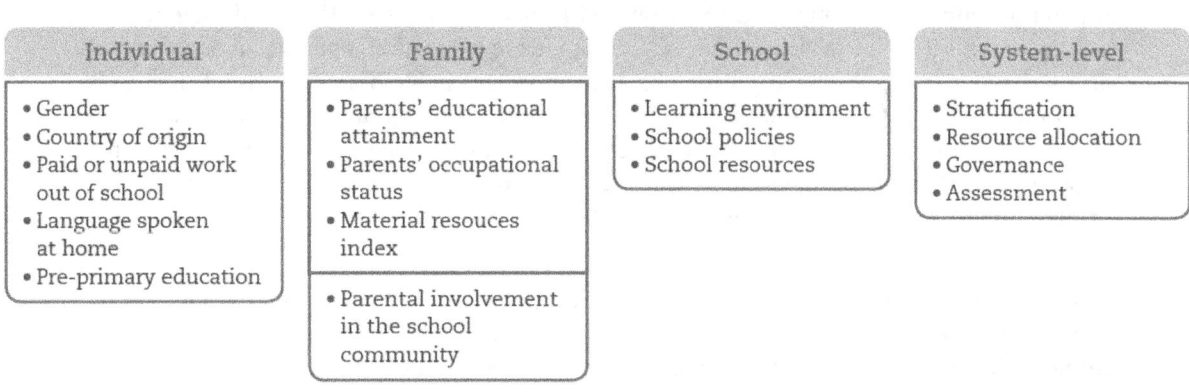

Source: OECD (2018[17]).

Despite a greater motivation to achieve, students with an immigrant background generally have not been able to capitalise on their motivation to achieve success in school. Even in some countries where academic underperformance among immigrant students is not as marked, analysis shows that students with an immigrant background exhibit comparatively poor outcomes on other measures of well-being, such as a strong sense of belonging at school, or high levels of schoolwork-related anxiety (OECD, 2018[17]).

Socio-economic disadvantage and language barriers are two of the greatest obstacles to the successful integration of students with an immigrant background. Immigrant students in OECD countries who do not speak the language of assessment at home are around eight percentage points less likely to be academically resilient than native-speaking immigrant students. In some countries though, the education system and the host communities help students with an immigrant background overcome disadvantage and enable them to capitalise on their high motivation to succeed and flourish (OECD, 2018[17]).

There is little research on refugee children, unlike the large body of research available on the children of immigrants. This is often linked to the fact that refugee children are not specifically identified or sampled in sufficient number in national or international surveys such as those by PISA enabling comparison of children of the same refugee groups across countries. This gap in research makes it difficult to reach any conclusion as to how refugee children perform in school across countries (Crul et al., 2017[18]).

While some research on the current wave of refugees is being carried out at the moment, research already exists on previous waves of refugees in Europe in the 1990s, when individuals fled from the former Yugoslavia, Iran, Iraq, Afghanistan and Somalia. A large body of research on refugee integration in school system is also available from Australia (Matthews, 2008[19]), Canada (Wilkinson, 2002[20]) and the United States (McBrien, 2005[21]). The limited data reveal that refugee children face more obstacles than other children of immigrants (SNIS, 2015[22]); (European Commission, 2013[23]); (McBrien, 2005[21]; Sirin and Rogers-Sirin, 2015[24]; Suárez-Orozco et al., 2011[25]).

Most research on the children of refugees has focused on the limited period after their arrival, when they attend welcome or introduction classes. In Greece for example, structures for the reception and the education of refugees provide pre-integration services, followed by reception classes that emphasise psychological support to smooth transition to mainstream education structures. However, it is important to examine the next steps after the welcome classes. Existing research has focused on singular factors, such as trauma or individual background (Nilsson and Bunar, 2016[26]). Institutional factors such as the organisation of welcome classes or language education and the availability of access beyond compulsory education are also important in shaping the school pathways and outcomes of refugee children, but have not received much attention in the literature (Crul et al., 2017[18]). Countries differ in how the education system is organised and what opportunities refugee children have to access and benefit from education and training opportunities. This variation can impact the academic and well-being outcomes of refugee children.

Access to education and an early starting age are important for promoting the integration of immigrant and refugee children (Crul et al., 2017[18]). Yet access is not guaranteed for refugee children in all countries, either before or after compulsory school age. An early starting age in education is key because gaps early on in education – especially in language acquisition – are only magnified later without appropriate countermeasures.

Findings from the Netherlands, for example, suggest that ten hours of language development per week provided to children 2.5 to 4 years old in day care centres and preschools reduces the difference in language and skills between advantaged and disadvantaged children (Akgündüz and Heijnen, 2018[27]; Leseman et al., 2017[28]).Disadvantaged children who attend day care centres and preschools implementing these programmes show higher language skills than disadvantaged children who participated in other centres and preschools (OECD, 2017[29]).

Furthermore, the number of contact hours in elementary school is important, since a greater number reduces the dependency on parents for support. Even with a sufficient number of contact hours, most refugee children experience gaps at the end of elementary school. Later tracking of secondary school children can help to close gaps over time. Options to move up from vocational to academic tracks (i.e. alternative or long routes) are also important. Refugee children often need to make use of alternative routes, and are often held back by second language problems due to their late arrival in the country of destination. Overall, second language learning and acquisition are key for this group of students. An extensive period (up to two years) in separate classes can hinder educational success; a quick transition into regular classes together with sustained second language support can be more effective. Alternatively, schools can combine separate and regular class hours to ensure that refugee children will also be in contact with children whose first language is the national language. Refugee children often need more time to adjust to the new education system and to their new life, which may be very different from their previous experience (Crul et al., 2017[18]). Additionally, they may have experienced several years of interrupted schooling in different transit countries, which also necessitates more time and more flexibility in the new education system.

While education systems can and should play a role in promoting the well-being of refugee students, their role should be seen in light of a broad and co-ordinated effort encompassing the education, health, social and welfare systems, potentially involving partnerships among schools, hospitals, universities and community organisations (OECD, 2018[17]).

What are the challenges related to housing for refugees and other vulnerable migrants?

Large inflows and rapidly changing numbers of incoming migrants seeking protection require a quick response to emergency housing needs. Providing adequate accommodation for asylum seekers and refugees – often with little time to prepare, and in some countries for a very large number of people – has been a costly challenge for many governments. Governments are also required to provide different forms of accommodation, as housing needs of asylum seekers and refugees change over time. Governments must quickly provide reception facilities, but this may not be adequate for settlement and needs may evolve, notably due to family reunification. Meanwhile vulnerable groups, for instance unaccompanied minors and victims of sexual violence, have special accommodation needs that must be considered. Also, different countries have different models for providing housing allowances and/or access to social rental housing.

The first stage is emergency reception. Aside from building temporary shelters – for instance in the form of container homes or tents – vacant buildings, military facilities and sports halls have been repurposed to react to an often great and sudden need for reception facilities. In some OECD countries, such as Austria, France and Germany, private hotels or camp groups are also used in the case of large inflows. Mostly, however, asylum seekers are accommodated in collective facilities (EMN, 2014[30]). Furthermore, most OECD countries have subcontracted NGOs and private companies to build or help run reception facilities. In the majority of EU countries, the central government is financing reception centres.

Problems of overcrowding, lack of privacy and other inadequate conditions such as those relating to sanitation have been recurrent issues, particularly in countries with very high numbers of incoming migrants such as Greece.

Authorities have put in place a number of strategies to increase preparedness and facilitate the building of reception centres or the repurposing of unused buildings. Prior to 2014, the majority of EU countries had emergency plans for reacting to large numbers of incoming migrants seeking protection. Since then, early warning mechanisms to monitor the capacities of reception centres and projections to anticipate future inflows are becoming more widespread in order to increase preparedness (EMN, 2014[30]).

Furthermore, a more even allocation of asylum seekers can be a means to decrease pressure in specific areas of the country. In Finland, Portugal, Switzerland, the United Kingdom and Italy, for instance, availability of reception facilities is factored into the dispersal of asylum seekers across the country (OECD, 2016[31]). However, this of course implies that reception centres still have the necessary capacity, or that innovative housing solutions are provided by the local stakeholders (Galera et al., 2018[32]).

In order to quickly build reception facilities or repurpose existing buildings, a number of countries – including Germany, Sweden and some of the States in Austria, have relaxed building codes such as energy efficiency requirements. Other countries, such as Sweden, tightened eligibility criteria to free up spaces in reception centres, for instance by not providing access to rejected asylum seekers with expulsion orders.

While overcrowding can only be addressed by increasing the overall availability of places, the quality of reception centres can be enhanced by introducing guidelines on how to run and design the facilities. For instance, the German Ministry for Family, together with UNICEF, has developed minimum safety standards for children, young people and women in reception centres and collective accommodation. These also include construction measures to ensure more privacy, spaces for children, and single-gender sleeping areas.

It is important for refugees to move out of initial reception facilities as soon as possible. Delays in the settlement process can hinder integration, particularly when refugees remain in reception facilities for a long time with limited or no access to integration activities or job opportunities (Hainmueller, Hangartner and Lawrence, 2016[33]).

Yet, quick transfer of recognised refugees from reception centres to more permanent housing has been challenging for many countries. In the Netherlands for instance, in early 2016 about 16 000 beneficiaries of protection were still in reception facilities for asylum seekers, because the municipality they were assigned to could not offer them housing. In 9 out of 24 EU Member States, including Austria, Belgium and Luxembourg, applicants who have received refugee status can stay in reception facilities for asylum seekers longer if they have no other housing options (EMN, 2015[34]).

Governments have recently implemented measures to speed up the transition of refugees from reception centres into municipal housing. The Dutch Government, for instance, requires municipalities with insufficient social housing to temporarily repurpose or lease buildings. Additional funding is provided by the central government for up to two years to give municipalities more time to find housing while reducing the pressure of reception centres and implementing integration measures earlier. In 2016, Sweden required municipalities to accept all refugees who have not found housing themselves and are referred to them through a central mechanism at the Public Employment Service. Previously, municipalities had considerable discretion in deciding whether they wanted to host refugees.

Refugees face the same structural difficulties as other people in finding affordable housing. In countries where housing supply is limited, new inflows generate pressure to increase the overall housing stock. Moreover, refugees may encounter discrimination in access to housing and doubts about their ability to pay rent.

Mainstream initiatives to facilitate access to housing for lower-income residents also benefit refugees and other vulnerable migrants. These include government demand-side subsidies, such as means-tested housing allowances, although these transfers may not be high enough to make housing affordable. Housing allowances were provided to refugees in 15 of 24 EU Member States surveyed in 2014, but amounts differed across countries and indeed were often insufficient to pay rent (EMN, 2015[34]). Public incentives may also focus on the supply side, e.g. tax incentives or subsidies for real estate developers. As there is little large-scale construction of social rental housing, the private sector plays a crucial role in increasing the supply of affordable housing (Salvi del Pero et al., 2016[35]). Public-private partnerships for affordable housing can be an opportunity to increase the supply of low-cost housing. However, finding the right incentives for private developers remains a challenge. In addition, assuring that such projects are economically viable in the long run and still meet the social and economic needs of low-income renters can be difficult, particularly when public funding ends after a certain point (Bratt, 2016[36]).

Settlement of asylum seekers and refugees compels authorities to align policy objectives that are often difficult to reconcile: quickly move migrants from reception centres to more permanent housing; provide housing at relatively low cost; distribute asylum seekers and refugees to areas with job opportunities while avoiding spatial segregation in disadvantaged neighbourhoods. This is true even if accommodation is not government-sponsored. Distribution is complicated by poorer local labour market conditions in areas where housing is cheaper (OECD, 2016[37]). Social rental housing has often been built in the peripheries of cities, partly mirroring the need to find low-cost land (Scanlon, Fernández Arrigoitia and Whitehead, 2015[38]). In a number of countries, moreover, housing shortages are particularly acute in urban areas, while asylum seekers and refugees gravitate to cities where they can find better employment opportunities and networks. The difference between urban and non-urban situations strongly correlates with migrant presence and integration outcomes.

What are the challenges related to the health of refugees and other vulnerable migrants?

Unexpected migration inflows place a great deal of stress on health systems in host OECD countries, requiring them to respond adequately to migrants' health needs. Health systems need to be resilient to adapt to an increase in the number of refugee patients often having multiple and complex health needs (OECD, 2018[39]).

The short-term response must be to provide asylum seekers and refugees with access to basic health services. In their country of origin or during the journey, most of them have been exposed to health risks, such as communicable diseases, poor sanitation, and lack of access to healthy food or safe water supply; any of these can lead to poor health outcomes.

Most asylum seekers and refugees have also experienced mental stress or severe psychological problems that may require strong psychosocial support: loss of relatives or friends along the way, trafficking, exposure to sexual violence or abuse, or disability related to war injuries. For example, at least half of the refugees in Germany suffer from some form of mental illness (Bundes Psychoterapeuten Kammer (German Federal Chamber of Psychotherapists), 2015[40]). A high level of anxiety disorder was also reported among those surveyed in the Greek islands in late 2016 and early 2017 (Médecins Sans Frontières, 2017[41]). The World Health Organisation (WHO) estimates that rates of depression, anxiety and poor well-being are at least three times higher among refugees than among the general population, and are increasing over time (Health Organization Regional Office for Europe, 2016[42]). For treatment of refugees' mental health problems to be successful, they must employ a multidisciplinary approach; be culturally sensitive or adapted for specific groups; use trained paraprofessionals; and be linguistically appropriate (Mental Health Commission of Canada, 2016[43]).

In light of their vulnerability and the right to health (Box 2.2), refugees should receive support. However, since many refugees (and recently arrived asylum seekers) are concentrated in specific areas and are often highly mobile, responses by health care services should be adapted.

Most OECD countries conduct health screenings when people apply for international protection. In some countries, screening is used to identify vulnerable persons, with special attention paid to children and pregnant women. In other countries, the purpose of health screening is mostly related to public health. Resettled refugees also go through medical examination in order to identify their eligibility and needs upon arrival.

In the medium term, the challenge is to ensure access to health care. Health systems need to remove practical barriers to care for asylum seekers and refugees. These barriers include limited entitlements, inadequate information, administrative obstacles (e.g., waiting periods or procedures for obtaining a registration number or fee exemption), the cost of treatment and/or medicine, limited availability of relevant health workers, and cultural and language mismatches. Providing relevant information about rules for access to care and available services will help refugees, asylum seekers and other vulnerable migrants access and use services appropriately and in a more timely manner.

Asylum seekers and refugees need to learn who to contact and where to go to depending on their needs. They have to adapt to the cultural environment of their host countries and understand the sharing of responsibilities among different categories of practitioners as well as among different levels of services.

Outreach services can provide assistance through information, support, referrals and advocacy. They are usually accessible (both financially and geographically), and they can help identify the health needs of newcomers and direct them towards the appropriate services. Social workers in outreach services are often familiar with the background of the population they support, and are often more trusted than mainstream health services.

Language can be a major barrier to care for asylum seekers and refugees: refugees with complex health needs may not receive sufficient information and may be less likely to participate in decision making. That could in turn reduce compliance with treatment and lead to mistrust between physicians and refugees.

Language barriers can be overcome through the use of local interpreting agencies, or by employing staff with a range of linguistic capabilities. A number of NGOs provide translators or cultural mediators – often refugees themselves – to overcome language and cultural barriers and facilitate access to health care. In some countries, public or private operators also provide medical practitioners with remote translating and interpreting services, which can improve the accessibility and quality of health care when interacting with refugees and other vulnerable migrants.

> **Box 2.2. Migrants' right to health**
>
> The migrants' right to health is generally guaranteed by national laws and in several international human rights documents. For refugees, the 1951 UNHCR Convention states that, "Refugees lawfully staying should receive the same treatment with respect to public relief and assistance as is accorded to nationals." When it comes to asylum seekers, the EU Reception Condition Directive states that, "Member States shall ensure that applicants receive the necessary health care which shall include, at least, emergency care and essential treatment of illnesses and of serious mental disorders."
>
> In practice, equal access is ensured for refugees in all OECD countries, but entitlements for asylum seekers vary widely across countries. Full access to health care is guaranteed to asylum seekers only in a few countries, while in some others they only have access to emergency care. In many countries, entitlements require that asylum seekers remain inside reception centres or designated areas.

Access to health care can also be hindered by staff availability, notably when reception centres are located in areas where access to health care is lacking for the general population. In such cases, availability of services may depend on the personal commitment and willingness of a few dedicated health workers.

In addition, training may be required to support the skills development of health workers in welcoming and servicing this new public. Lack of knowledge among frontline staff and managers with regard to entitlements, cultural differences and specific health needs should also be addressed, together with the negative perception of asylum seekers in the media and the local population.

The long-term response should be to anticipate future shocks and long-term needs. The key to providing resilient health services lies in the ability to transform service provision and organisation so as to be able to plan for those needs. Health systems must re-evaluate their long-term ability to absorb and efficiently treat the health requirements of future refugees.

A co-ordinated response is necessary for a country to better anticipate and prepare for future shocks. The 2016 Strategy and action plan for refugees and migrants, signed by WHO Member States, was a first step on this path (WHO Regional Committee for Europe, 2016[44]). A whole-of-government approach will allow co-operation among health institutions, humanitarian and regional bodies, but also among non-governmental institutions, private companies, international organisations and other countries. The health needs of migrants and refugees should be fully integrated into existing health structures and legislations.

Through training, future generations of health care professionals can adapt their practices to the needs of refugees and other vulnerable migrants. In order to do so, courses on the health rights of migrants and their specific vulnerabilities as well as intercultural courses could be included in standard medical and nursing curriculum. Such courses already exist in several universities in OECD countries but are rarely mandatory.

Easing and accelerating recognition of foreign credentials for refugee health care professionals would allow them to contribute to their host society. Numerous refugees are highly trained; some are qualified doctors, nurses or pharmacists. With appropriate accreditation and training, these professionals could contribute to addressing the needs of both the host and refugee populations. Refugees are well represented in the health care sector across OECD countries but not necessarily at their right level of qualification. In 2014, 15% of refugees aged 15-64 were employed in the health and social work area, against 10% of the native-born population in the European Union (EU/OECD, 2016[1]).

In all OECD countries many health care professions are regulated, and recognition of the foreign professional qualification is mandatory to ensure that quality standards are met. A registration, certificate or licence awarded by a professional licensing body is a prerequisite to being able to practice. These regulations are meant to protect the health and safety of populations by ensuring that professionals meet the required standards of practice and competency. Although recognition procedures tend to be long and expensive, some countries have speeded up procedures for the entry of skilled immigrants into the health care sector (OECD, 2017[45]).

Health systems responded appropriately in most cases to the recent large inflows of refugees, and no serious issue of public health safety was recorded. Still, there are many areas for improvement.

The first area is the short-term response and the capacity of health systems to service mobile populations. En route support was not available except from NGOs, which had to develop action plans for Europe for the first time. The lack of co-ordination among stakeholders at different stages of the asylum process sometimes led to inefficient service delivery. Triage according to health needs worked only for the most severe cases and left many people, notably those with mental health problems, falling between the cracks.

The second area for improvement has to do with access to health care during the asylum process and for recognised refugees. Despite theoretical access in most countries, a number of administrative, financial and language barriers remain.

In the long run, better integration of migration and health services as well as an appropriate training of health professionals is needed to make sure that the bottlenecks faced by health systems in some OECD countries are overcome in the future. Again, there is also scope to better use the competencies of refugees with experience in the health sector.

What challenges do unaccompanied minors face?

One group facing an indisputable situation of vulnerability is unaccompanied minors, children who migrate without parents or caregivers and find themselves in the host country. As their number has increased in recent years, they have become a major policy challenge. Between 2014 and 2016, European OECD countries received more than 180 000 asylum applications from unaccompanied minors, and the United States reported almost 170 000 border apprehensions of unaccompanied minors. In 2015-16, UNICEF recorded at least 300 000 unaccompanied minors in around 80 countries, almost five times more than the 66 000 registered in 2010-11 (UNICEF, 2017[46]). The vast majority of unaccompanied minors are boys aged 16 to 17 with very little prior education.

Young unaccompanied minors are often among the most determined to build a new life in their host country. Yet these children face extensive challenges in adapting to that new life, and often need substantial and urgent help to find their way through the school system and into the labour market in a meaningful and durable way.

All young migrants face challenges upon arrival in their host country: learning the language and integrating into school; catching up with their native-born peers; and qualifying for further education. Young unaccompanied minors, without a parent or guardian to provide them with emotional, financial, logistical, social or psychosocial support, face additional challenges.

Further, unaccompanied minors are more likely than other young migrants to have special health and mental health challenges. These children have often been travelling for months or years, in unhealthy, unsafe and stressful conditions. They are at higher risk of psychosocial difficulty, behavioural problems, negative role modelling and substance abuse. This endangers their integration prospects and can increase delinquency.

As mentioned, unaccompanied minors – like other young migrants – often have difficulties integrating into school, particularly when the education system in their home country differs from that in their host country. Indeed, research indicates that while it takes children approximately two years to acquire communicative language skills, it can take them up to seven years to develop the academic language used in school environments (OECD/EU, 2015[13]). Unaccompanied minors do not have the time to catch up; most arrive at an age when their peers in host countries are close to completing or have completed compulsory education. They have little time to learn the host country language and take on new content before they face the tests that determine eligibility for further education (this also applies to refugee children older than age 15).

A further challenge is that job-search intensity is high among unaccompanied minors. Many want to work – and start earning – soon after arrival, hoping to remit money back to their family, which may have spent everything to fund their journey. While employment motivation bodes well, it can prevent investment in longer-term integration through continued education, and lead unaccompanied minors to be stuck in low-skilled and unstable work.

Guidance from an early stage and throughout the asylum application and integration process is important for the long-run outcomes of unaccompanied minors. Timely appointment of a guardian not only can reduce the number of children going missing from care - willingly or unwillingly - soon after arrival, but also can provide psychological stabilisation, build trust and protect the child. There is no standard definition across OECD countries of the roles and responsibilities of the guardian; indeed, the mandate, tasks and qualifications vary widely. Despite this, a number of factors have emerged as central to a well-functioning guardianship system:

Although the guardian plays a central role, children should be provided with information about procedures and available options at each step, so that they can influence their integration path.

The initial reception period is particularly important. While there is no universal model, and individual needs should be addressed, three key points about reception can be identified.

First, detention of minors should be avoided, since it has serious and long-term detrimental effects on their psychological and physical well-being and their development.

There are alternatives to detention – including residence restrictions, open facilities, regular reporting, electronic monitoring and surrender of passport.

Second, processing times should be accelerated to minimise time spent in temporary reception facilities, to start integration quickly and free up space. In some countries demand for a place in a shelter remains high: in November 2017 for example, there were twice as many unaccompanied minors waiting for a place in a shelter in Greece than were available.

Third, based on assessment of the children's needs and circumstances, a range of care arrangements should be available, such as semi-independent supervised living, small group homes and foster care. Resources should be allocated based on needs: some children only require a few services or only for a limited time. Vulnerability criteria should be harmonised – nationally or even regionally – to target support.

Integrating young migrants – especially late arrivals – in school is a challenge requiring targeted support (Box 2.3). OECD countries have pursued a number of approaches to facilitating the transition from migrant to student for those who arrive near compulsory school-leaving age. Efforts in this direction include orientation classes, basing class assignment on skills and knowledge assessments, and extending the school-leaving age. Since unaccompanied minors arrive unpredictably and throughout the school year, it can be difficult to find education and training programmes they can immediately join if they do not arrive at the beginning of a term. Responses to this challenge could be to create bridging programmes to prepare them for entry into vocational training at the start of the next term.

Box 2.3. Unaccompanied minors in schools

The main challenge for host country education systems is to enrol unaccompanied minors in school as soon as possible. Many of these children have long been out of school, and further delays in enrolment should be avoided. Although European Union Member States must ensure the access of asylum-seeking children to education within the first three months of their arrival, delays are common, for two reasons. First, formal education is rare during long stays in reception centres (EU-FRA, 2016[47]). Second, after moving to a care facility, a shortage of places and lengthy procedures may delay enrolment for several months. In addition, in some countries age-related restrictions might make enrolment difficult or even impossible.

Unaccompanied minors also require further support to ensure their successful integration into schools (OECD, 2018[17]). Additionally, many unaccompanied minors often arrive when they are older and cannot be integrated as easily into the education system as young children. In some cases they enter the vocational training system instead, if they are eligible. This eligibility can depend on asylum-seeking minors being granted a work permit following a transitional period.

Source: (OECD, 2018[17]).

Integrating unaccompanied minors when they have left school can be more challenging still. Tailored career guidance should help young migrants understand the long-term implications of their early educational choices. In addition, some OECD countries have developed programmes – such as the Education Contract in Sweden – that facilitate continuing education alongside work, enabling unaccompanied minors to earn and send remittances to their families while continuing their education (OECD, 2016[48]).

Transition into adulthood is a sensitive question in the treatment of unaccompanied minors in OECD countries. Many unaccompanied minors reach adulthood while their asylum cases are still pending, at which point many OECD countries reduce or withdraw the additional protection applied to them as children. This abrupt change is particularly problematic when the children are unprepared and taken by surprise; in such countries, they should be prepared for it in advance and be informed about the different strategies that can be taken (EMN, 2018[49]).

An abrupt end in support at age 18 can undermine previous integration efforts; indeed, evidence from Sweden shows that the risk of abandoning education and training is especially high when leaving care. A more effective model allows young adults to gradually transition from one protection system to another, receiving continued support where individual needs remain. Such continued support is available in a number of OECD countries, including Germany, Sweden and France. In those countries, an extension of the support offered to minors can be requested for a limited time – usually up to three years, or until the age of 21.

What specific challenges do refugee women face?

Refugee women are a sizeable and growing group. According to data from Eurostat, about half a million women obtained international protection in Europe since 2015, 300 000 of them in Germany. In Europe in 2014, women numbering 800 000 comprised 45% of those declaring to have arrived for reasons of international protection. Whereas the early flows of asylum seekers in Europe during the 2015-16 humanitarian crisis were predominantly men, the share of women has risen over time. Globally, women are more likely than men to obtain protection when they apply for asylum; the share of women among those obtaining international protection status has increased from 29% in 2015 to 38% in 2017. The presence of refugee women is expected to rise further through family reunification, as the majority of spouses concerned are women.

Refugee women are particularly vulnerable. Previous OECD work (OECD, 2006[50]) has shown that immigrant women face a "double disadvantage" – that is, they have poorer outcomes compared to either immigrant men or native-born women. What is more, in over two-thirds of OECD and EU countries, immigrant women have larger gaps with respect to employment in relation to their native-born peers than do immigrant men. Immigrants tend to be disadvantaged due to the fact that they have generally been raised and educated in a very different environment and (often) language. Refugees face additional challenges related to the nature of their forced migration, such as health issues, weak prior links with the host country, and often a lack of documentation of their education or work experience (OECD, 2016[31]). Refugee women are thus a priori at a particular disadvantage, as they have to tackle the specific obstacles facing immigrants, refugees, and women at the same time. This raises the question of whether there is a "triple disadvantage", i.e. whether the challenges related to gender, immigrant status and forced migration add up, or even reinforce each other.

An OECD report (Liebig and Tronstad, 2018[51]) provides an overview of the outcomes of refugee women in select EU and OECD countries, and discusses certain key issues with respect to the integration challenges facing refugee women, building on evidence from a number of OECD countries with large refugee intakes.

Recent OECD research (OECD, 2017[52]) has shown that the integration of immigrant women is decisive for the integration outcomes of their children, to a greater extent than what is observed for native-born mothers and children. In particular, the labour market status of immigrant mothers has a strong positive impact on the employment prospects of their children, especially their daughters. Given the high returns from refugee women acquiring language and education, there is a strong case for investing in their integration.

The report (OECD, 2017) finds that compared to refugee men, women take a longer time to get established into the labour market. Whereas men experience relatively steep gains in employment rates during the first 5-9 years after arrival that then taper off, the integration path of refugee women is characterised by modest but steady increases that continue for at least 10-15 years. Refugee women also have lower levels of host country language skills compared to men in the first 2-3 years after arrival. While the gap gradually closes over time, language proficiency remains at lower levels.

Refugee women with intermediate or advanced levels of proficiency in the host country language have employment rates 40 percentage points higher than those with little or no language skills. Once accounting for socio-demographic characteristics, the difference is halved but remains much stronger than for other migrant women.

Compared with both refugee men and other migrant women, refugee women experience a stronger increase in their employment rate when they have higher qualifications. However, 40% of those with tertiary education who found a job were overqualified – twice the figure of their native-born peers.

When employed, refugee women are frequently in part-time employment. In European OECD countries, more than 4 out of 10 employed refugee women have a part-time job – almost twice the level among native-born women, and six percentage points more than among other immigrant women.

For refugee women, the likelihood of becoming pregnant increases in the year after arrival, as the uncertainty and insecurity experienced prior to and during the process of flight makes them more reluctant to have children during that period. Possible waiting periods for family reunification may further stoke the unfulfilled desire to have children. The peak in fertility shortly after arrival slows integration of some refugee women.

A number of recommendations can be drawn from these findings. There is a strong link between refugees' employment and their social network, especially contacts with the native-born, but women have far fewer networks than men. Mentorship programmes can help create such networks.

Compared with refugee men, refugee women frequently receive less integration support, both in terms of hours of language training and in connection with active labour market measures. Evidence from Sweden suggests that specific attention paid to refugee women in introduction activities results in a positive effect on employment.

Waiting periods abroad could be used for pre-departure integration measures (for example, engaging in language education), but this rarely happens. Other initiatives for the integration of family migrants can be directly applied to refugee women (Box 2.4).

There is a need for more flexible arrangements regarding the timing and organisation of introduction activities; these arrangements should take account of the specific needs of women with small children – otherwise support will be given when it is less likely to have an effect on outcomes. Flexible language course arrangements for mothers also provide good results in terms of outcomes.

> **Box 2.4. Integrating refugee women who arrive in the context of family migration**
>
> The majority of refugee women have arrived in a context of family migration – either accompanying their refugee husband or joining him later. This implies that their integration bears similar challenges and policy responses as that of family migrants. The OECD recently published a summary of good practices with respect to the integration of family migrants (OECD, 2017[53]), which are depicted in Figure 2.6.
>
> **Figure 2.6. Key practices to favour integration of family migrants: Lessons from ntegration reviews in OECD countries**
>
>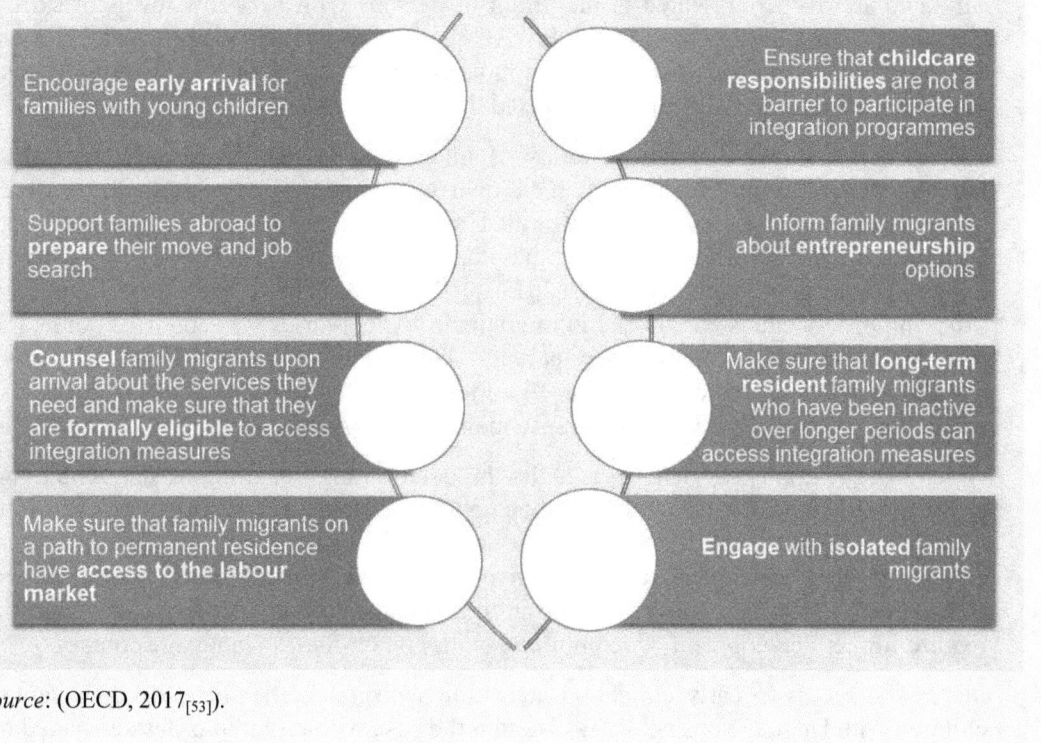
>
> Source: (OECD, 2017[53]).

How do very low-skilled refugees and other vulnerable migrants fare in terms of integration?

A low skill level is one of the main factors affecting integration prospects. The less-educated population in many OECD countries is disproportionately composed of migrants. This makes them more vulnerable because low-skill migrants are more likely to be illiterate than low-skill natives. People illiterate in their own native language face particularly steep challenges in accessing the labour market. Mainstream integration and activation programmes are generally ill-suited to less-educated and especially illiterate individuals. There are so few illiterate natives in most OECD countries that activation programmes no longer take this group into account.

In addition, there are fewer jobs for the low skilled. For example, in Sweden the number of low-skilled jobs is declining; very few native-born persons work in low-skilled jobs; and the demand to fill these jobs is weak, yet the proportion of the foreign-born population whose highest education is primary or pre-primary is nearly 10 percentage points higher than among the native-born population (OECD, 2016[48]). This creates more competition among the low skilled for the few jobs available.

On average, the employment outcomes of less-educated migrants are better than those of less-educated natives. In Europe the outcomes are identical; however, this is mostly due to the relatively poor outcomes of less-educated natives. Less-educated refugees fare much worse than other less-educated migrants.

On average, migrants are less proficient in literacy, numeracy and problem solving than native-born adults in all countries participating in the Survey of Adult Skills (PIAAC), although skill levels vary across countries (Box 2.5).

Migrants are over-represented in the group of persons with very low levels of skills, as measured among those who take the PIAAC reading components assessment. There is a large gap among immigrants, depending on whether they speak the host country language and on the country in which they completed their education.

Past evidence shows that the difficulty of integrating low-skilled immigrants into the labour market has less to do with their own outcomes and more with those of their children, especially in Europe. Low-skilled immigrants' children face a higher risk of poor school and labour market outcomes than the children of low-skilled natives and higher-skilled immigrants (OECD, 2017[52]; 2017[54]). The employment rate of the offspring of less-educated non-EU immigrants in EU countries was about 12 points lower than that of persons with native-born parents. There is an important difference by gender: female native-born children of non-EU immigrants outperform their male peers in education, whereas the inverse is the case in the labour market.

Given the centrality of language skills in determining integration and employment prospects in the host country, the development of effective and tailored language tuition is critical. Migrants with little daily exposure to their host country language also tend to be less efficient language learners. Effective language tuition, therefore, will also involve supporting employers to work with and in turn support individuals whose language skills require further development, by combining work and on-the-job language courses.

Increasing access to early childhood education with a specific focus on disadvantaged children with language obstacles – as is often the case with children of less-educated non-EU immigrants – not only would allow the mothers to enter the labour market, but also would likely provide high returns for the children themselves; this was demonstrated by evidence from a number of OECD countries such as France (OECD, 2008[55]). Many OECD countries have specific policies in place to help children of immigrants with language obstacles, often based on systematic language screening in preschool coupled with follow-up remedial classes (OECD, 2018[17]).

One way to support refugees with low education levels is to assess informal skills. Skills that a refugee possesses should be recognised to the extent possible. Integration policy can play an important role in this, giving prospective employers an important signal about the skills that foreign-born and foreign-trained adults hold (OECD, 2017[45]).

Since low-skilled refugees and vulnerable migrants have difficulty following integration measures developed for people with higher education levels, they cannot be expected to benefit from mainstream programmes that do not take their skill level into account. Integration programmes tailored to this group – and to illiterate persons – are more effective.

Box 2.5. Widespread low literacy proficiency among migrants

One-third of migrants reach at most Level 1 in literacy in the Survey of Adult Skills, twice the number of natives who are at or below Level 1 (OECD, 2018[10]). The share of adults with a medium level of literacy skills (Level 2) is similar for the two groups.

Large differences also exist between migrants and natives and across countries in the share of persons with very low literacy levels. In all countries except Chile, migrants are over-represented among persons who reach at most Level 1 in literacy proficiency (Figure 2.7). At this level, persons can read brief texts on familiar topics and locate specific information in them, but are not able to extract information from longer and more complex texts. The situation differs sharply among countries. The share of migrants with a very low level of literacy proficiency is highest in Turkey (70%). In a number of European countries (France, Italy, Spain, Slovenia and Sweden) as well as in the United States, 40% or more of the foreign-born have a very low literacy proficiency level. In contrast, less than 20% of migrants in Ireland, Australia, the Czech Republic and New Zealand have a very low level. Migrants are six times more likely than natives to have a very low literacy proficiency level in Sweden; four times in Finland and Norway; close to three times in Denmark, Germany, the United States, Belgium (Flanders) and Austria; and twice as likely in France, Slovenia, the United Kingdom (England and Northern Ireland), Canada and Estonia.

Figure 2.7. Adults with very low literacy proficiency (Level 1 or below), by country of birth

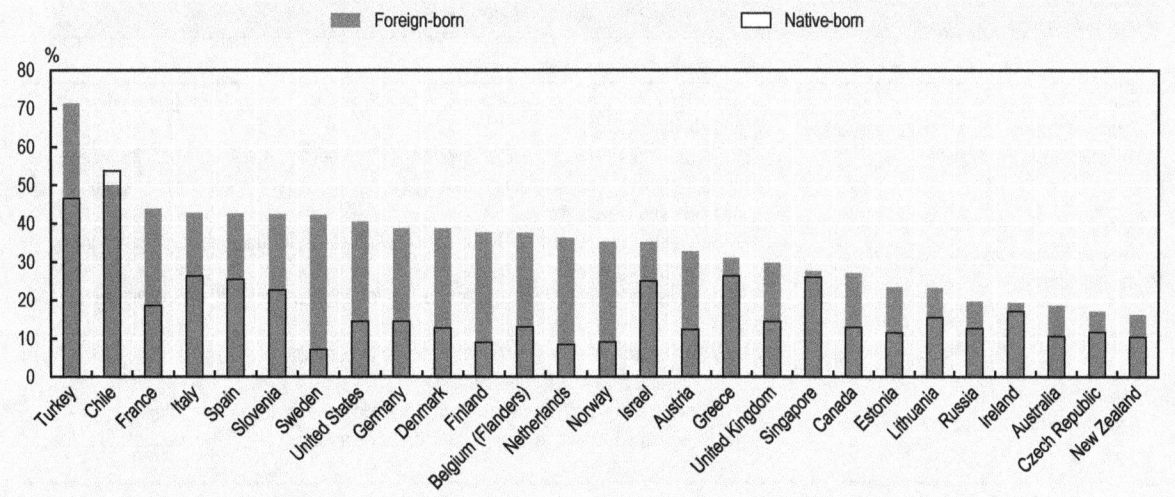

Note: The sample includes persons aged 16-65. Belgium only covers Flanders; the United Kingdom only covers England and Northern Ireland.
Source: OECD (2018[10])

How can multilevel governance contribute to successful integration in host countries?

When integrated successfully, refugees and other vulnerable migrants contribute to their local communities in many ways. However, the size and composition of migrant communities vary greatly across regions and cities. Maximising the opportunities for integration requires taking into account the specificities of migrant populations, as well as the economic, social and geographic characteristics of the host countries, regions and cities. Policies that are co-ordinated across levels of government and institutions, and that include the contribution of non-state actors, can ensure that integration measures are adapted to local realities.

Based on the findings of a study with a territorial perspective on migrant and refugee integration, which came from a survey of 72 European cities and 9 in-depth case studies (OECD, 2018[56]), the OECD proposed a Checklist (Table 2.1) of public action for migrant integration at the local level featuring twelve Objectives for policymakers gathered around four pillars. Cities report having experienced some gaps in multi-level governance in responding to the recent inflows of asylum seekers and refugees. New inter-institutional arrangements have been adopted to contribute to integration in some countries of settlement.

Table 2.1. Checklist of public action for migrant integration at the local level

Pillar 1 Multi-level governance: Institutional and financial settings	1: Enhance effectiveness of migrant integration policy through improved vertical co-ordination and implementation at the relevant scale. 2. Seek policy coherence in addressing the multi-dimensional needs of, and opportunities for, migrants at the local level. 3. Ensure access to, and effective use of, financial resources that are adapted to local responsibilities for migrant integration.
Pillar 2 Time and Space keys for migrants and host communities to live together	4. Design integration policies that take time into account throughout migrants' lifetimes and status evolution. 5. Create spaces where the interaction brings migrant and native communities closer.
Pillar 3 Capacity for policy formulation and implementation	6: Build capacity and diversity in civil service, particularly in key services receiving migrants and newcomers. 7: Strengthen co-operation with non-state stakeholders, including through transparent and effective contracts. 8: Intensify assessment of integration results for migrants and host communities and their use for evidence-based policies.
Pillar 4 Sectoral policies related to migration	9: Match migrant skills with economic and job opportunities. 10: Secure access to adequate housing. 11: Provide social welfare measures that are aligned with migrant inclusion. 12: Establish education responses to address segregation and provide equitable paths to professional growth.

Source: (OECD, 2018[56]).

The challenge most frequently highlighted by the cities surveyed was a lack of adequate co-ordination with central government on integration policy and implementation. Official competencies at the local level have shifted in many OECD countries in recent years, with responsibilities for integration and reception of refugees and other vulnerable migrants devolved or centralised. Enhancing multi-level co-ordination could also ensure that persons with specific needs (women at risk, children – especially unaccompanied minors – victims of trauma, trafficking or sexual violence, persons with disabilities and elders) receive adequate assistance as early as possible.

Multi-level governance tools can influence local policy makers' performance towards integration, orient their priorities, and build capacities. Such tools could include platforms for dialogue and information sharing; incentives for co-ordination; priority selection based on performance achievement; contracts and indicators for integration results and policy implementation formulated jointly across levels of government; and *ex post* evaluation.

Lack of cross-sectoral co-ordination among different policy fields, in particular housing, education, employment and health, was also highlighted as a city level concern. Local integration-related initiatives are often designed in silos, particularly in large cities. This can lead to fragmented integration policies and may create bottlenecks in delivery. Policy co-ordination through a local strategy for inclusion, the creation of shared information systems and practices, and through building a sense of shared responsibility among all departments that deal directly and indirectly with refugees is particularly important for vulnerable migrants with multiple service needs. A number of cities have begun to put in place mechanisms, such as milestones that each department must achieve, that move in the direction of ensuring more inclusive public services.

Nearly half of the surveyed cities identified capacity gaps (described as insufficient know-how, training, and capacity – technical as well as infrastructural – of local actors to design and implement integration policies) as a significant challenge facing local integration policy. Capacity building among public service providers (and their subcontractors) can be an important tool to ease the language and cultural barriers that compromise access to public services among newly arrived refugees and other vulnerable migrants.

While some central governments set national standards for access to universal services for refugees, the implementation of these standards frequently remains the responsibility of lower levels of government. Reliance on municipal efforts alone, however, is unlikely to be sufficient. Municipal efforts must be combined with national monitoring and evaluation to ensure capacity building is implemented where it is most needed.

Mismatch between socio-economic and administrative boundaries, or implementation at the wrong geographic scale, may impede integration policies. Implementation of key integration-related services, such as housing or psychological support, will often require co-ordination across neighbouring localities, as well as across regions, in order to reach the right target group and cover the relevant basin.

Communicating local strategies is an important tool for fostering participation and collaboration, and for avoiding the social tension that sometimes accompanies large migration inflows. Further tools to strengthen information sharing across levels of government – including consultations, standard setting and monitoring of integration indicators – can clarify responsibilities among different stakeholders, strengthen transparency, and help gain the support of public opinion.

The vast majority of cities sampled collaborate with NGOs on projects related to integration. More efficient partnership can be achieved through dialogue mechanisms, the use of contracts which leave margin for NGOs to react to changing circumstances, clear standards, as well as transparent monitoring and bidding procedures.

National reception and integration mechanisms for asylum seekers and refugees have been accompanied in most cases by resources transferred to the municipal level, either as a lump sum in relation to the number of asylum seekers and refugees received in the city, or as recovery costs for the services that were paid by municipalities up front (Box 2.6).

Municipalities, however, frequently express concern that funding is insufficient. In many countries this has led to reluctance on their part to accept to host refugees – which will have a negative impact on early integration prospects.

Further, in many OECD countries the short-term direct costs of refugee integration faced by municipalities largely focus on financing early integration measures and/or language training; if integration is not fully successful, the long-term costs can be substantial (OECD, 2016[48]). This is particularly true for less-educated refugees who may have a longer pathway to integration.

Box 2.6. Financing integration at the local level

Fiscal transfers have become the main instrument for central governments to fund rising integration costs at the sub-national level. Still, payments generally cover only a fraction of the actual costs of receiving sub-national governments (OECD, 2017[53]).

Since the educational composition of refugees tends to vary considerably within countries, the budgetary implications of settlement can also vary substantially. In the majority of OECD countries, however, the funding transferred to municipalities for refugee settlement is independent of both local cost considerations and the characteristics of those refugees settled.

In a number of countries, municipal reimbursement is determined on the basis of costs. In Finland for example, alongside a fixed reimbursement component for the first three years following settlement, municipalities are reimbursed on an explicit cost basis for the provision of services such as municipal integration measures, interpretation, and welfare provision. With the exception of unaccompanied minors and those requiring long-term health and social care, the duration of cost reimbursement is independent of the characteristics of the migrants or their likely integration speed.

Source: (OECD, 2017[57]; 2018[58]; 2017[59]).

Can entrepreneurship facilitate integration of refugees and other vulnerable migrants?

One of the most commonly used measures of entrepreneurship activities is self-employment. The self-employed are defined as those who own and work in their own business (OECD, 2017[60]). Some work alone while others have employees.

In most OECD countries, immigrants are more frequently self-employed than the native-born population. In 2015, for example, 19% of working immigrants in the European Union were self-employed, while the share among the native-born population was 14% (Figure 2.8).

Immigrants are, however, a very heterogeneous group that includes highly skilled workers, family migrants, students, and vulnerable groups such as refugees. Accordingly, self-employment activities vary greatly across these groups in terms of scale and quality. For example, evidence from Canada shows that refugees are less likely to be self-employed than the native population during their first three years in the new country, but the proportion who are self-employed doubles after five years and exceeds that of the native population (Green et al., 2016[61]).

Figure 2.8. Self-employment rates of immigrants and natives by country, 2015

Self-employed as a percentage of total employment (15-64 year-olds)

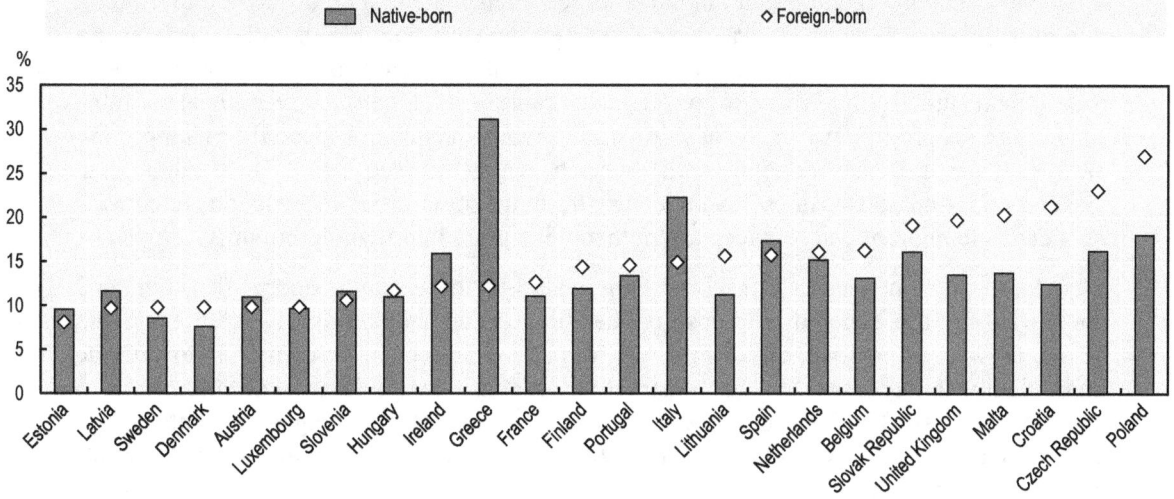

Source: Special tabulations of 2015 Eurostat Labour Force Survey.

Refugees who wish to start a business face a number of barriers (OECD, 2018[62]). First, they may lack the entrepreneurship and language skills needed to launch a successful business venture. These include technical skills (e.g. written and oral communication, problem solving); business management skills (e.g. goal setting, decision making, finance, negotiation, customer relations); and personal entrepreneurial skills (e.g. risk management, change management, strategic thinking, leadership) (OECD/The European Commission, 2013[63]). Entrepreneurs from refugee groups often lack many of these skills, particularly competencies related to management (Rath et al., 2011[64]; Hiebert, 2009[65]).

One area where refugees are particularly challenged is in language abilities, which creates a barrier when navigating new regulatory and institutional regimes to launch a business (Rath et al., 2011[64]; Hiebert, 2009[65]). Similarly, language difficulties can make it more difficult to apply for loans and start-up capital and to look for business partners. The development of customer and supplier relations is also more challenging. One way for refugee entrepreneurs to get around this challenge is to set up a business that focuses on customers from the same community, and to seek suppliers that speak the same language (Rezaei, Goli and Møballe, 2006[66]).

Difficulties apart from language may also be encountered in accessing start-up finance, lack of which is one of the most frequently cited barriers to business creation for all entrepreneurs. This barrier is likely greater for refugee entrepreneurs, who may have a short-term residency status and lack savings, credit history or collateral (Betts, Omata and Bloom, 2017[67]). Refugee entrepreneurs therefore often turn to informal funding mechanisms, such as securing financing from family members and acquaintances, or using rotating savings and credit associations (Rezaei, Goli and Møballe, 2006[66]). However, these funding mechanisms are often limited to relatively low amounts since they are essentially cash-based systems. Thus the majority of refugee entrepreneurs who access these informal financing systems when starting a business are often forced to downsize their business plans.

Many cities and regions offer courses and workshops in business start-up and business management for entrepreneurs from refugee groups. These courses cover the typical issues that would be expected in training for any entrepreneur, including business and financial planning, taxation and human resource management. The difference in training for refugee entrepreneurs is that these offerings typically include modules on business culture and societal issues. Training sessions are often offered in various languages to make them attractive and relevant to refugee entrepreneurs. One such example is the four-stage "!gnite" programme in Sydney, Australia, which has been successful in supporting new start-ups and also reducing social security payments (see Box 2.7). In addition to business start-up and business management training, some cities offer language courses that can help migrant and refugee entrepreneurs integrate into their community.

Coaching and mentoring can provide business start-up and social supports. Coaching and mentoring are professional relationships that support the acquisition of entrepreneurship skills, as well as personal development. The role of the coach or mentor is to provide individually tailored advice and constructive feedback to guide the entrepreneur in a learning process. The key to success for the provision of coaching and mentoring to refugee entrepreneurs is to quickly establish trust, so that they seek professional support rather than advice from their family or personal networks (OECD, 2018[62]). This can be accomplished by offering support in various languages and from members of their community.

The development of community-based financial mechanisms and self-funded communities can also be supported with training and support in setting up their infrastructure. There has recently been a revival of community-based financing systems, particularly in southern European Union countries. In Spain, for example, this is most visible through the growth of the Associació de Comunitats Autofinançades (ACAF, or Association of Self-Funded Communities), a non-profit organisation that fosters the creation and development of these communities.

> **Box 2.7. !gnite, Australia**
>
> The !gnite Small Business Start-ups initiative is a support programme for newly arrived refugees in Sydney. First there is a meeting with the individual to assess their entrepreneurial potential. Participants then work with an advisor to identify skills needs and appropriate training sessions. They are also matched with a mentor and are invited to networking sessions. When the business is launched, the entrepreneurs are supported in building websites, developing promotional material and completing basic bookkeeping. In the final stage, support is scaled back and referrals to other business support systems are provided.
>
> Two hundred and forty clients were accepted into the programme over three years and 61 new businesses were created. An evaluation found that the programme's financial and human resources were not sufficient to help all clients as needed. Nonetheless, the programme is considered a success because clients improved their English and expanded professional and social networks, and social security payments were reduced (Collins, 2016[68]).

Finally, including entrepreneurship programmes in local policies for integration can also help refugees access resources needed to start or develop new businesses. Cities have traditionally acted as hubs for kick-starting entrepreneurs, including migrants; they can help migrants overcome different obstacles in establishing their activities, such as lack of knowledge about the culture and regulatory environment for business creation and self-employment. They do so by offering integrated packages of entrepreneurship support, including language training and business management training (OECD, 2018[56]).

What can be done to engage employers to hire refugees and other vulnerable migrants?

Employers play a key role in the integration of refugees and other vulnerable migrants: if they are not willing to hire refugees or face too many hurdles in the process, getting refugees into employment will be difficult to achieve. Given employers' key role of providing jobs and training opportunities, it is crucial that integration policies are attuned to employers' skills needs and that policy frameworks facilitate reaching out, hiring and retaining refugees in companies through a streamlined and easy-to-follow process.

The role of employers in the integration process often goes beyond ensuring refugees' economic independence and has other, positive side effects. Working alongside native-born co-workers can boost language skills, increase social interactions among different groups, and ultimately tackle stereotypes and prejudice.

While employers cannot and should not be expected to replace publicly provided integration services, their contributions are crucial to complement public policy efforts. At the start of the recent refugee surge, there was little documentation or analysis of the obstacles employers face when seeking to hire refugees, what their motivations are for doing so, and how public policy could best support them.

The OECD and UNHCR developed a 10-point multi-stakeholder action plan for employers, refugees, governments and civil society (Box 2.8). The ten points are described below.

Box 2.8. The OECD-UNHCR Action Plan for Engaging with Employers in the Hiring of Refugees

UNHCR – the UN Refugee Agency – and the OECD launched an action plan in April 2018 to expand employment opportunities for refugees (www.unhcr.org/5adde9904). The action plan was based on a series of regional dialogues with employers in Nordic countries, German-speaking countries and North America, as well as at the EU level. These consultation rounds, held between 2016 and 2017, and a survey among German employers on hiring refugees conducted in 2016 served as the foundation for identifying a number of key obstacles and policy responses to assist employers.

Correctly assessing and interpreting skills of refugees is often difficult for employers due to language barriers, lack of documentation of education and skills, and difficulties in interpreting foreign diplomas when they are available. Employers, particularly small and medium enterprises, may not be willing to take the risk of hiring a candidate whose professional skills are difficult to assess. Thus, rendering skills more transparent would increase the employability of refugees and facilitate employers' hiring decisions. This requires governments to develop and expand the availability of existing skills assessment tools, facilitate the recognition of foreign diplomas, and invest in tools to assess skills acquired informally. Many OECD countries have highly formal labour markets and limited experience in assessing and validating informal skills. Yet many refugees have work experience in the informal sector, making validation of these skills an important field for policy development in the coming years.

Building language skills and providing opportunities for professional upskilling are necessary next steps, not only to ensure that job candidates match employers' skill needs, but also to facilitate long-term integration into the economy. Employers usually require good or very good language skills from job candidates. Evidence from a survey among German employers shows that around half of them demand at least good German language skills, even for low-skilled positions. For medium-skilled jobs, this share of employers rises to 90% (OECD, 2017[7]). Generally, stronger language skills are associated with better labour market outcomes; on average in the EU, refugees who state that they speak the host country language on an intermediate level have double the employment rate of those who declare they have the language skills of a beginner or less (EU/OECD, 2016[1]). It is therefore important to ensure that language courses cater to different learning needs and capacities. Upskilling measures such as additional training courses, vocational education and adult education also allow potential skill mismatches to be addressed, particularly in countries where few employers are in need of low-skilled labour.

Finding qualified refugee candidates is a challenge for many employers. Refugees often lack the networks that can introduce them to employers or provide job leads. Furthermore, job counsellors in public employment services often have limited experience in identifying the skills of refugees and matching their profiles with employers. Job fairs, online job platforms and civil society organisations that work with refugees are essential for bridging this divide. Closer co-operation between public employment services and employers could streamline the placement of qualified candidates into jobs, particularly if public authorities train staff to cater to specific needs of refugees.

Navigating the administrative and legal framework can be difficult for employers, especially when job applicants are asylum seekers. In many OECD countries, complex legal frameworks govern hiring asylum seekers or refugees as employees, apprentices or interns. Understanding regulations, obtaining work permits and going through bureaucratic procedures can pose a considerable disincentive for employers. Procedures for work permits should be streamlined and regulations consistently implemented across the country. In addition, step-by-step guidance and individual information should be easily accessible to employers, for instance through dedicated websites or information hotlines.

Ensuring sufficient legal certainty for employers is essential to facilitate refugee employment. Even when administrative procedures are manageable, employers may be unwilling to offer jobs to refugees whose perspectives of being allowed to stay in the country are uncertain. Employers may be reluctant to make an investment in additional apprenticeship or job training. Ensuring that apprentices are allowed to remain in the country during the period of training could mitigate that reluctance. More broadly, governments should be aware that issuing short-term residence permits diminishes employers' readiness to hire refugees.

Helping employers to create a more inclusive workplace can prepare the working environment for new refugee employees, and is also an opportunity to assess whether the company's policies addressing discrimination and harassment are sufficient. An inclusive work environment welcomes new hires and has supervisors and colleagues with the skills to address possible language barriers and resolve potential misunderstandings related to different workplace behaviours or communication styles. In addition, senior management should clearly establish expectations towards new and established staff, communicate the company's rationale for hiring refugees and actively involve their staff, e.g. through mentorship schemes. In many countries, employers' associations and civil society organisations provide guidance and training to employers on intercultural communication, non-discrimination and inclusive management practices.

Ensuring that integration support continues once refugees have been hired is crucial, particularly for low-skilled refugees and for those who entered the labour market through internships or short-term contracts. Work can be combined, for example, with further education, professional training or language courses. Such measures can help turn initial placements into more stable and productive employment. Furthermore, employers may be more willing to hire refugee workers who do not yet have all the necessary skills for the job if training and upskilling measures are available throughout employment. During the consultation rounds for the OECD-UNHCR action plan (Box 2.8), many employers noted that ongoing training was often not available and expressed a wish for more support after hiring refugees, such as having a contact point at public employment services.

Given the large number of actors involved in integration policy, many countries have faced challenges in co-ordinating actions and policy responses; this has sometimes led to regulations frequently changing or implemented with a delay or unevenly across the country. When it is difficult to understand the responsibilities of different actors and where to go for support and information, employers are discouraged from engagement. Better co-ordination is necessary among employers, public employment services, local immigration authorities and governments, as is enhanced collaboration with education providers and connection with civil society initiatives.

Many employers do not see a business case for hiring refugees, and many of those who do were motivated by a sense of social responsibility (OECD, 2017[7]). This motive may not be robust in ensuring employment in the long run, particularly in times of economic downturn. To build a stronger business case, it is essential to strengthen refugees' skills and their productivity, make it easier for employers to hire refugees, and mitigate risks and uncertainty.

How can the contribution of civil society be fully harnessed in integrating refugees and other vulnerable migrants?

While it is the responsibility of governments to ensure the availability of integration services, the third sector plays a crucial role in the integration process and in many OECD countries has been at the forefront of supporting newly arrived, vulnerable migrants (OECD, 2017[69]).

The third sector encompasses a wide array of actors and institutions – ranging from local volunteer initiatives to (international) NGOs, migrant associations, third sector organisations including social enterprises, and non-profit service providers who receive government funding to implement welcome and integration services. Given this diversity, the role that the third sector can and should play greatly depends on the professional and financial capacity of the respective actors, their role at the local level and the engagement of the local community (Galera, Giannetto and Noya, 2018[70]).

Furthermore, how integration of vulnerable migrants is organised differs considerably throughout the OECD area. In France, Germany, Italy and Greece, for instance, the third sector is historically strongly involved in the first phases of reception, providing for instance emergency accommodation and supporting the processing of asylum requests. In other OECD countries, first reception is predominantly organised and implemented by government authorities.

In addition, some countries have a long-standing tradition of delivering integration services through professional, non-profit service providers, e.g. in the resettlement process in the United States and Canada (OECD, 2016[31]). In other countries, integration services are predominantly delivered by government institutions and agencies, with the third sector regarded more as a complementary actor. However, in practice their role is often greatly enhanced when government provisions cannot be rolled out quickly enough or fail to cover all circumstances, areas or types of vulnerable migrants (OECD, 2016[31]). Third sector organisations have also recently experimented with innovative integration pathways that are not limited to work integration but have a broader focus on social and cultural dimensions (Galera, Giannetto and Noya, 2018[70]).

Regardless of national differences in how the integration process is organised, the involvement of volunteer initiatives, migrant organisations, NGOs and social enterprises is essential in facilitating the integration of vulnerable migrants. By operating on the ground and engaging with migrants and local populations, they are well positioned to provide direct insights and feedback on whether policies work in practice and how integration measures could be adapted to better address the needs of vulnerable migrants. This however also implies that there need to be structures in place that allow for such feedback loops, for instance through regular consultation rounds between governments and third sector representatives.

Furthermore, volunteer initiatives that foster interactions between locals and new arrivals not only are important to foster social cohesion overall, but also in boosting language skills and accelerating migrants' transition into the labour market. There is strong evidence that access to social and professional networks helps job seekers obtain leads and increases their likelihood of finding employment (OECD, 2017[52]). One-on-one mentorship programmes can be a cost-effective way to facilitate integration of vulnerable migrants with limited networks, provided that such schemes set clear objectives and train mentors to support vulnerable migrants adequately (OECD, 2007[71]; 2008[55]). Large-scale programmes have been developed by the third sector in a number of countries, including Canada, Denmark, New Zealand and Norway.

Migrant associations should be a key interlocutor for policy makers when the latter design, implement and evaluate integration policies, in order to ensure that provisions actually respond to needs and that policy makers understand group-specific hurdles that may exist in accessing support measures. Migrant associations can provide a unique insight into what works in practice and why; also, particularly among vulnerable migrants, they more are likely to be perceived as a trusted contact point because language barriers are less of an issue.

However, most OECD countries have had difficulty harnessing the full potential of the third sector in facilitating integration. Particularly in reaction to the influx of asylum seekers, a plethora of NGO and civil society initiatives have sprung up in European

OECD countries, and co-ordinating these different actors and integration offers has been a challenge for governments. In some cases, co-operation has been impeded by differing political aims. Nonetheless, a number of original initiatives have triggered innovative socio-economic integration pathways (OECD, 2016[31]).

Moreover, many integration services initiated by civil society groups, NGOs and non-profit service providers are financed through national governments. Funding periods are often short, which can lead to a quick build-up of capacity that later goes unused once project funding has run out. Setting up more sustainable funding structures with built-in evaluation mechanisms is crucial in order to increase effectiveness and professionalism of the third sector. Innovative funding mechanisms can also help address the issue of resources (Box 2.9).

> **Box 2.9. The social impact bond – A new model for funding integration?**
>
> Since 2016, Finland has been piloting a new model for integration with the aim of speeding up the integration process. Training modules are interspersed with employment, so participants are able to undertake periods of work followed by top-up integration training to fulfil needs as they emerge, rather than prior to starting work. Target sectors include construction, services, care, ICT, restaurants and catering.
>
> What makes this initiative particularly innovative is the funding model, a "social impact bond". Companies were invited to invest in a private fund used to finance the educational and work programmes undertaken as part of the pilot project. Investors receive a return on their investment if the costs associated with the labour market integration of participants are lower than those of a comparable group who do not receive the new training. Investors – rather than the public sector – bear the financial risks involved in testing this novel approach. If the employment objectives are met, the Finnish Ministry of Economic Affairs and Employment will pay a portion of the savings into a fund from which the investors can draw their initial capital as well as a "reasonable" profit. Private funding was necessary for the pilot, since random assignment to publicly funded programmes is not possible in Finland – public initiatives must be open to all users.
>
> *Source:* (OECD, 2018[58]).

Furthermore, while the involvement of local volunteer initiatives has been key to responding to the integration of newly arrived vulnerable migrants, expecting volunteers to take over tasks that are the responsibility of the state is not going to be viable in the medium or long run. Vulnerable migrants are often in a very complex personal, social and legal situation, and volunteers may not be adequately equipped to respond to such complex needs. Investing in the capacity of volunteers is therefore important, but the right balance must be found between supporting volunteers and continuing to offer professional, high-quality public services. Ensuring that volunteers are not overburdened will also render citizen engagement more durable in the long run.

Lastly, few OECD countries have managed to systematically involve migrant associations and harness their know-how when either implementing or designing integration policy. While this may imply investing in the capacity building of migrant associations, it also requires a more fundamental shift in policy making that designs integration measures not only *for* migrants, but also *with* them.

What is the impact of channels of entry on the integration of refugees and other vulnerable migrants?

Not all refugees and other vulnerable migrants enter in the host country through the same channels, and the channel of entry makes a difference. Refugees arriving as asylum seekers generally have little time to prepare and no contact with the destination country prior to arrival. Candidates for resettlement are selected from a roster, and vetted and prepared for their resettlement, but selection is usually from among the most vulnerable candidates. Other vulnerable migrants are able to use complementary legal pathways for migration to destination countries.

Resettlement presents an opportunity to provide support prior to arrival, at arrival, and in the integration phase that follows. It refers to the transfer of refugees from an asylum country to another state that has agreed to admit them and ultimately grant them permanent settlement. While refugees arrive with a secure status and access to social services and the labour market, they themselves do not select this country. Only a small number of states take part in resettlement programmes. While the United States has been the world's top resettlement country cumulatively, Canada, Australia and the Nordic countries also resettle a considerable number of refugees annually. Some non-traditional countries of resettlement have also been stepping up their programmes, such as Chile, Japan and Korea (see Box 2.10).

Box 2.10. The Japanese resettlement programme

Refugee resettlement in Japan began with the acceptance of Indochinese refugees in 1978. Besides convention refugees, the Japanese Government accepted 11 300 Indochinese refugees from 1978 to 2005. Resettlement assistance was delegated by the government to the Refugee Assistance Headquarters (RHQ). Refugees could stay in RHQ facilities, participate in four months of Japanese language education and life-skills classes, and receive employment assistance (vocational guidance, job placement, public vocational training, etc.).

These measures have continued after the end of acceptance of Indochinese refugees. Japan accepts refugees based on a Cabinet agreement about the Resettlement Program. From 2010 to 2014, the country accepted 86 Myanmar refugees from camps in Thailand, and from 2015 accepted Myanmar refugees from Malaysia, for a total of 174 refugees through 2018 (Ministry of Foreign Affairs of Japan, as of September 2018).

RHQ provides refugees arriving in Japan a 180-day resettlement support programme with 572 hours of Japanese language education, 90 hours of lifestyle guidance, and employment assistance that includes consultation, job placement and workplace training. After the programme, resettled refugees can receive follow-up support. Assistance is also provided by NGOs that help refugees with application procedures, accommodation, medical care, language education and employment assistance.

The annual quota and criteria for selection of refugees are based on a political decision in each resettlement country. Nevertheless, persons' need for protection and the absence of any lasting durable solution are the main eligibility criteria. States additionally accord priorities to additional criteria, such as the refugees' potential for economic and social integration. The United States, which resettled almost 54 000 refugees in 2017, resettles those who fit into at least one vulnerability category (such as women and girls at risk, survivors of violence or torture, people with urgent medical need, and children at risk). Hence, resettled refugees differ from asylum claimants because they do not choose the country where they are settled; they are likely to be more vulnerable; and they are more likely to be women, girls and families with children, compared to other refugees.

For those selected on the basis of vulnerability, low education levels and health issues are associated with lower labour market outcomes compared to refugees entering through the asylum system. Analysis of the long-term labour market outcomes of resettled refugees is scarce, since data on admission class are not available in most countries. A Swedish study suggests that resettled refugees have the lowest and slowest employment attachment, compared to asylum applicants and family reunion immigrants (Bevelander, 2011[72]).

For resettling refugees, the pre-departure period can be used for pre-arrival integration measures and better subsequent planning. UNHCR interviews and submits refugee cases to countries for resettlement consideration; subsequently, under co-operative agreements with those same countries, the International Organization for Migration (IOM) provides case processing, health assessments and pre-departure orientation. Upon arrival, resettlement countries provide refugees with legal and physical protection, including access to civil, political, economic, social and cultural rights similar to those enjoyed by nationals. Resettlement also means the opportunity to eventually become a naturalised citizen. Successful resettlement depends on strong partnerships to assist individuals and families to start a new life in a new country (ICMC, 2011[73]).

Unlike asylum claimants, resettled refugees are settled in a local community directly upon arrival and do not stay in asylum centres before actual settlement. This means that resettled refugees in general have limited knowledge about the host society, culture or language upon arrival. To assist the resettled refugees it is important to develop integration policies in consultation with the relevant national and local stakeholders (ICMC, 2011[73]). Involving municipalities, NGOs and other actors in preparations for the arrival of refugee groups, and providing them with relevant information on the refugees' backgrounds and needs, are crucial to link the different phases of the resettlement process. Extensive planning and information sharing is necessary to ensure that important needs, including health needs, are met upon arrival. During the first phase of resettlement, refugees require intensive and personalised support to navigate the complex systems and services of the resettlement country. This support should be limited in time and in accordance with individual needs.

In general, resettled refugees cannot choose the place of settlement within their new host country, but are assigned to a municipality by the government. In most countries the decision to settle refugees in a given municipality depends on the willingness of the municipality in question. In other countries, such as Denmark and the Netherlands, municipalities are obliged by law to receive a certain number of refugees per year. Many resettled refugees are settled in smaller communities outside the largest cities. Research suggests that settlement in smaller communities actually makes it easier for resettled refugees to build social networks and to connect with the new host community (Klaver and van der Welle, 2009[74]). Nevertheless, to scatter resettled refugees in isolated areas with very limited employment opportunities and a hostile community can be problematic and lead to further relocation (secondary migration).

> **Box 2.11. Agricultural partnership programme for resettled refugees in the United States**
>
> The Office of Refugee Resettlement (ORR) provides short-term cash and medical assistance to new arrivals, as well as language classes and job readiness and employment services, to facilitate refugees' transition in the United States. ORR supports additional programmes beyond the first eight months post-arrival, including microenterprise development, ethnic community self-help, agricultural partnerships, and services for survivors of torture. One of these programmes is the Refugee Agricultural Partnership Program. RAPP has a dual aim: to improve the supply and quality of food in urban and rural areas through refugee farming projects; and to provide resettled refugees with sustainable or supplemental income and better physical and mental health.
>
> *Source:* "The U.S. Refugee Resettlement Program – an Overview", www.acf.hhs.gov/orr/resource/the-us-refugee-resettlement-program-an-overview.

Complementary international protection pathways for beneficiaries – which include labour, international study and family migration channels as well as private sponsorship – can improve the likelihood of good outcomes for those who are able to use them. Labour migration channels are generally employer-driven, and so newly arrived migrants are already in employment. International study channels resolve the obstacle of foreign, unrecognised and unfamiliar qualifications and also address the language skills shortfall, although the latter depends on the language of instruction. Family migration channels ensure that the migrant arrives in a family that is to some degree settled, since eligibility criteria for sponsorship often include income and other integration requirements. Private sponsorship can make a major difference in integration outcomes due to the immediate network of support that provides the sponsored individual with benefits such as access to mediation, services and resources, and employment opportunities.

How can first asylum, transit and destination countries be supported in integrating refugees and other vulnerable migrants in host communities?

A large majority of the world's refugees – 85% at the end of 2017 – are concentrated in developing countries. In fact, nine out of the top ten countries to host refugees are low- or middle-income countries. Four countries – Lebanon, Uganda, Pakistan and Turkey – together host 36% of the world total. Syrian refugees constitute 98% of the refugees in Turkey, while the refugee population in Pakistan almost exclusively originates from Afghanistan. In total, over one-quarter of all refugees live in low-income countries with limited resources to cope with the direct and indirect costs induced by refugees.

Refugees are concentrated in low-income countries that are disproportionately affected by conflicts and other humanitarian crises. The reason is that most people forced to leave their home do not necessarily wish or have the means to travel long distances, and therefore often seek refuge in countries neighbouring their own – which frequently are also poor countries.

Although most refugees remain in developing countries for the duration of their displacement, many later move on to seek asylum in OECD countries, and may pass through several "transit countries" before reaching their final destination.

Many refugees and other vulnerable migrants in those developing transit and destination countries live either in UNHCR camps or other reception facilities. At the end of 2017, outside OECD destination countries, almost half of all refugees lived in camps or other collective reception facilities (UNHCR, 2018[75]).

In developing transit and destination countries, access to basic living conditions is a significant challenge for refugees and other vulnerable migrants. They are indeed more likely to face very poor living conditions after a forced displacement, which often induces a loss of financial assets as well as trauma. Due to their fragile legal status, they may also lack access to specific rights.

Integrating forcibly displaced people into host communities in developing countries is fraught with challenges, some of which could be overcome with greater coherence between humanitarian, development and peace actors. This "triple nexus" is the subject of a forthcoming OECD DAC Recommendation on Humanitarian-Development-Peace Coherence.

Historical efforts to "link" relief, reconstruction and development have not lived up to expectations. In addition, donors and host countries may have different definitions of "success": international actors tend to push for local integration, while host countries often prefer repatriation (OECD, 2017[76]). In most fragile and conflict-affected states, which often host large numbers of refugees and internally displaced persons, donors may prioritise emergency aid over long-term development programmes due to perceived risks.

Political, legal and practical issues also need to be considered, including the political will of the host country to grant refugees the right to work; differing interpretations of the right to free movement; the lack of identity documents; and language barriers. These limit job opportunities, integration into the education system, and opportunities for social cohesion. Several recent policy initiatives have taken a holistic approach based on partnerships between governments, humanitarian organisations and development agencies (Box 2.12).

Box 2.12. The Jordan Compact

The Jordan Compact is a long-term funding and planning strategy in that country" aimed at providing economic opportunities for refugees and vulnerable Jordanians. Launched in 2015 in collaboration with the European Commission, it aims at creating 200 000 working permits for Syrian refugees. The intention is to stimulate job growth through liberalisation of trade with the EU and promote investment in Special Economic Zones (OECD, 2017[77]).

The Jordanian Ministry of Labour has waived fees and some documentation requirements to facilitate access to formal employment for Syrian refugees. In February 2017, the Ministry granted Syrian refugees living in camps the right to obtain permits to work anywhere in the country. In August 2017, the ILO and UNHCR jointly established the Zaatari Employment Office, which offers job-matching services for camp residents, provides them with information on training opportunities and counselling, and allows refugees to register work permits (UNHCR, 2017[78]).

Where opportunities for return or integration at the regional level are scarce, displaced populations may resort to secondary movement, seeking entry into countries where they believe they will have access to protection and assistance (OECD, 2017[76]). Integration in the host country is therefore critical. In order to support developing countries in their integration of refugees and other vulnerable migrants in host communities – as called for in the Global Compact on Refugees – it is important to bring together the right amount of finance and use the right tools over the right time frame while providing the right incentives for stability – especially in countries affected by conflicts and other humanitarian crises.

Donors should work with states and partners to improve the access to rights by affected populations. This entails progressive advancement towards greater enjoyment of all rights until a comprehensive durable solution is reached. Comprehensive solutions have legal, economic, social, cultural, political and civil dimensions, all of which need to be addressed for solutions to be sustainable.

Donors and partners should work together from the onset of a crisis to develop strategies that define the long-term vision of a solution and the changes needed to achieve it. The approach should be a multi-year commitment, collaborative and inclusive, and involve a range of actors including refugees and IDPs themselves. Table 2.2 provides a framework for donors to measure progress towards comprehensive solutions for local integration, and a non-exhaustive list of indicators.

It is important to assess when situations are "ripe for resolution". Some of the prerequisites for comprehensive solutions include leadership to help identify, plan and move the solution forward; the availability of one or more durable solutions accessible to the displaced population; responsibility sharing by donors; political will in countries of origin and asylum; and external factors that can facilitate a solution, such as political change or peace processes. Donors can provide support to peace efforts by facilitating political dialogue.

Realising comprehensive solutions for displaced populations will require increased transparency in the planning, implementation and evaluation of processes around durable solutions like integration, return, reintegration and resettlement. Donors should also provide opportunities for complementary legal pathways in their support for comprehensive solutions.

Table 2.2. Progressing towards comprehensive solutions for local integration

Dimension	Description	Indicators
Legal	Refugees and IDPs enjoy a progressively wider range of rights and entitlements. This may lead to acquisition of permanent residence rights and ultimately the acquisition of citizenship in the country of asylum.	• Freedom of movement • Issuance of travel documents • Issuance of residence permits and work permits • Documented citizenship • Permanent residency
Economic	Refugees and IDPs can participate in the local workforce either through jobs or through self-employment, commensurate with their skills, and obtain a standard of self-sufficiency that is similar to the host country population.	• Right to work • Access to land • Access to financing or credit • Access to livelihood training • Access to professional licences and/or work permits
Social and cultural	Refugees and IDPs are accepted by the host community and state without fear of discrimination, intimidation or repression, and are able to create and maintain social bonds and links within the host community, participating fully in social and cultural life.	• Intermarriage • Establishment of joint businesses • Access to community centres • Representation of the ethnic, racial or linguistic groups in national and civil society media • Access to national services, e.g. education and health
Civil and political	Refugees and IDPs are increasingly able to participate in civil society, including in community governance and local and central government, as well as in election processes and public consultations.	• Participation in community leadership structures • Opportunity to vote • Inclusion in conflict prevention and peace building processes

Source: (OECD, 2017[76]).

What have we learned about reintegration in the home country of former refugees and other vulnerable migrants?

The displacement of people fleeing conflicts, natural disasters or economically deprived areas has put increasing pressure on receiving countries. While many asylum seekers who arrived in recent years have received or will receive at least temporary protected status, a significant number of requests have been or will be rejected. As a result, the number of migrants in OECD countries without a lawful residence permit and required to return has grown. In 2014, 200 000 asylum applications were rejected in first instance decisions; in 2017 this number had grown to over 500 000. Beyond rejected asylum seekers, other vulnerable migrants – such as victims of trafficking and unaccompanied minors – seek to return to their home countries.

Amid growing public anxiety and concern for the enforcement of the rule of law, destination countries have a compelling interest facilitating the safe and sustainable return of irregular migrants and others wishing to return to their origin countries, when local conditions allow. To date, these efforts have largely amounted to negotiating readmission agreements with the origin and transit countries of irregular migrants and so-called Assisted Voluntary Return and Reintegration (AVRR) programmes; AVRR involves funding and operational support for individual returns, often implemented in co-operation with NGOs and international organisations. The number of beneficiaries of AVRRs conducted by the International Organization for Migration (IOM) more than doubled between 2014 and 2016, from 43 700 to 98 400, mirroring the spike in asylum applications and irregular migration pressure in Europe in 2014-15. While decreasing by almost one-third to about 72 200 in 2017 as a result of a lower volume of voluntary returns from European countries, the figures remained significantly higher than in the 2005-15 period, pointing to a lasting trend (IOM, 2018[79]). The 2017 renewed action plan of the European Union (European Commission, 2017[80]) aimed at further increasing the return rate, which has remained relatively stable since 2008 at around 40% (Figure 2.9).

Being able to predict the demand for assisted return is also important. The EU Joint Research Centre (JRC) has developed an "Asylometer" which tracks, for each nationality and each Member State, the proportion of asylum applicants per country of nationality; the proportion of pending asylum decisions; and the rejection rate of asylum cases. The Asylometer is meant to compare the asylum situation across Member States and can help estimate resources that need to be allocated to support returns. The European Asylum Support Office has also developed a system for monitoring asylum-related migration (EASO, 2017[81]).

Although return of irregular migrants is an essential element of migration policy, returns from most OECD countries are still relatively rare. Further, AVRR – in spite of the name – is usually used by those who are required to leave and does not generally prompt a return decision (OECD, 2008[82]). Many voluntary return programmes are targeted at migrants residing irregularly in the host country, including visa overstayers or rejected asylum claimants. Yet even for migrants required to leave the country, voluntary returns are an attractive alternative to forced returns for host countries because they facilitate repatriation to countries with which no readmission agreement has been signed, and the return is simpler and less costly than removal. Some OECD countries therefore make substantial use of AVRRs. Germany recorded about 30 000 returns in 2017. Greece and Belgium were also among the top host countries for AVRR returns (IOM, 2018[79]).

AVRR is usually judged successful if there is no (re-)migration after return. Yet sustainable return means that migrants are successfully reintegrated in their home country, which includes social, economic and cultural dimensions. For this reason, indicators of successful return should not be based on the number of returnees but rather on the success of reintegration initiatives.

There are many factors determining reintegration outcomes, and not only the state of the home country. Reintegration can be seen as the outcome of the interplay of the returnee's individual resources and factors, and of institutional factors and arrangements. The latter is where policy action can be most effective.

Among the individual factors, the willingness to return is a key determinant of reintegration outcomes. Even poor living conditions in the destination country do not necessarily lead rejected asylum seekers to seek return if the situation in the country of origin is seen as unsuitable. The capability of migrants to return and reintegrate rests upon the economic and political situation in the home country, especially if the returnees left for humanitarian reasons. If the country of origin is peaceful and safe for the returnee, reintegration is more likely to succeed.

The willingness to return also depends on the relationship of the returnee with the home community. Barriers to return such as shame and a perception of failure can be counteracted only by support from families and local communities. Policy interventions and reintegration programmes therefore need to work with the home communities to build support and enhance their understanding for the returnees' situation.

Working with local communities is also necessary if returnees benefit from support that is not available to the rest of the population, to avoid resentment from neighbours who never migrated.

Other individual factors such as age, gender, education and marital status can also determine reintegration outcomes. For example, women may find it more difficult to establish a livelihood than returning men, particular if they are without close family members. Depending on local labour market needs, skills are not valued to the same extent in all regions, especially between urban and rural areas. Many reintegration programmes focus on supporting entrepreneurial activities of returnees, but individual skills and the local economic situation play a large part in whether efforts to find work are successful.

Figure 2.9. Number of third country nationals ordered to leave, persons returned, and the return rate (%) in the European Union, 2008-16

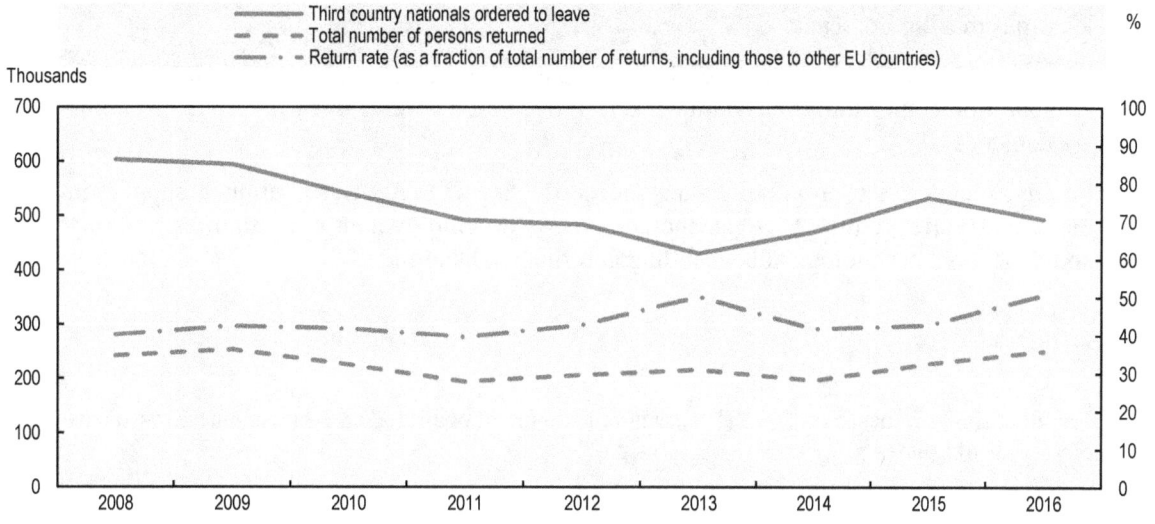

Source: Eurostat, 2018.

There are further group-specific factors affecting reintegration outcomes. In cases of religious or ethnic tensions, reintegration needs to take place in zones where there is less risk of exclusion of and discrimination against the returnee. Lastly, individual migration experiences impact reintegration. Victims of trafficking may fear reprisals and need support to avoid re-victimisation (IOM, 2015[83]). Unaccompanied minors need to reconnect with their families and pursue education or training. Both groups may need medical and psychological help.

Institutional settings in both the home and the host country largely impact reintegration outcomes. Co-operation between origin and destination countries on reintegration must reconcile divergent policy objectives. When there are many cases of return to manage, as well as a large number of refugees to protect and integrate, destination countries may find it hard to muster funding and public support for longer-term reintegration programmes. Strategic thinking on how to respond to those whose protection claims were rejected has begun to advance in the past three to five years.

For origin countries – particularly less developed countries and those that face a large influx of returning migrants, reception and reintegration of returnees also present challenges, notably in terms of absorption capacity and public opinion. Receiving and reintegrating returning emigrants may therefore have a relatively low priority, especially when the national context is politically or economically unstable. With high unemployment at home, states are less keen on receiving returnees, particularly when they arrive with little financial capital or low skill levels. Situations where returnees are openly ignored by the state or civil society are even more problematic. This applies to migrants that were already marginalised before emigration, but also to migrants who are seen as having failed to make it in the destination country. Lastly, a number of countries with large diaspora communities have begun to be actively involved with their returning migrants, offering reintegration support to enhance their impact on the local economy and society. However, most of these efforts are directed at migrants other than refugees (i.e. students and migrants with substantial work experience abroad). Reintegration programmes that specifically target refugees and other vulnerable migrants are still mostly offered by international organisations or development agencies, and not by the countries of origin themselves. To reduce the risk of conflict between home-country local populations and returnees, support efforts must take into account the populations in return localities that did not leave.

Reintegration can be considered early in the asylum process, such as through providing reintegration counselling to asylum seekers in reception centres even before their claims are decided.

Finally, reintegration programmes are more effective if they offer continued support in the country after return. This can include advice on employment opportunities, training and education, psychological counselling and financial support.

Note

[1] Student skills are based on PISA (Programme for International Student Assessment) assessments of 15-year-old students.

References

Akgündüz, Y. and S. Heijnen (2018), "Impact of Funding Targeted Pre-school Interventions on School Readiness: Evidence from the Netherlands", *De Economist*, Vol. 166/2, pp. 155–178, http://dx.doi.org/10.1007/s10645-018-9314-2. [27]

Åslund, O., L. Hensvik and O. Skans (2014), "Seeking Similarity: How Immigrants and Natives Manage in the Labor Market", *Journal of Labor Economics*, http://dx.doi.org/10.1086/674985. [16]

Betts, A., N. Omata and L. Bloom (2017), "Thrive or Survive: Explaining Variation in Economic Outcomes for Refugees", *Journal on Migration and Human Security*, Vol. 5/4, pp. 716-743. [67]

Bevelander, P. (2011), "The Employment Integration of Resettled Refugees, Asylum Claimants, and Family Reunion Migrants in Sweden", *Refugee Survey Quarterly*, Vol. 30/1, pp. 22-43, http://dx.doi.org/10.1093/rsq/hdq041. [72]

Bonfanti, S. and T. Xenogiani (2014), "Migrants' skills: Use, mismatch and labour market outcomes – A first exploration of the International Survey of Adult Skills (PIAAC)", in *Matching Economic Migration with Labour Market Needs*, OECD Publishing, Paris, http://dx.doi.org/10.1787/9789264216501-11-en. [11]

Bratt, R. (2016), "Affordable Rental Housing Development in the For-Profit Sector: A Case Study of McCormack Baron Salazar", No. March 2016, Harvard Joint Center for Housing Studies, Cambridge, http://jchs.harvard.edu (accessed on 14 November 2018). [36]

Brücker, H. (2016), *Forced migration, arrival in Germany, and first steps toward integration*, https://www.bamf.de/SharedDocs/Anlagen/EN/Publikationen/Kurzanalysen/kurzanalyse5_iab-bamf-soep-befragung-gefluechtete.pdf?__blob=publicationFile (accessed on 15 February 2018). [4]

Brücker, H., N. Rother and J. Schupp (2017), *IAB-BAMF-SOEP-Befragung von Geflüchteten 2016*, http://www.diw.de/sixcms/detail.php?id=diw_01.c.574033.de (accessed on 17 September 2018). [6]

Bundes Psychoterapeuten Kammer (German Federal Chamber of Psychotherapists) (2015), *BPtK-Standpunkt: Psychische Erkrankungen bei Flüchtlingen*, https://www.bptk.de/uploads/media/20150916_BPtK-Standpunkt_psychische_Erkrankungen_bei_Fluechtlingen.pdf (accessed on 31 August 2018). [40]

Collins, J. (2016), *From Refugee to Entrepreneur in Sydney in Less Than Three Years*, UTS Business School, https://www.ssi.org.au/images/stories/documents/Ignite/SSI_Ignite_evaluation_report_2017.pdf. [68]

Crul, M. et al. (2017), "The multiplier effect: how the accumulation of cultural and social capital explains steep upward social mobility of children of low-educated immigrants", *Ethnic and Racial Studies*, Vol. 40/2, pp. 321-338, http://dx.doi.org/10.1080/01419870.2017.1245431. [18]

EASO (2017), *Quantitative assessment of asylum-related migration: a survey of methodology*, Publications office of the European Union, Luxembourg, http://dx.doi.org/10.2847/642161. [81]

EMN (2018), *Approaches to Unaccompanied Minors Following Status Determination in the EU plus Norway: EMN Synthesis Report*, European Migration Network, Brussels, https://ec.europa.eu/home-affairs/what-we-do/networks/ (accessed on 14 November 2018). [49]

EMN (2015), *Integration of beneficiaries of international/humanitarian protection into the labour market: policies and good practices Synthesis Report for the EMN Focussed Study 2015 Based on the National Contributions from 24 Member States*, European Commission, https://ec.europa.eu/home-affairs/sites/homeaffairs/files/what-we-do/networks/european_migration_network/reports/docs/emn-studies/emn-studies-00_integration_of_beneficiaries_of_international_protection__eu_2015_en_final.pdf (accessed on 14 November 2018). [34]

EMN (2014), *Synthesis Report – The Organisation of Reception Facilities for Asylum Seekers in different Member States*, https://ec.europa.eu/home-affairs/sites/homeaffairs/files/what-we-do/networks/european_migration_network/reports/docs/emn-studies/emn_second_focussedstudy2013_oganisation_of_reception_facilities_final_version_28feb2014.pdf (accessed on 04 September 2018). [30]

EU/OECD (2016), "How are refugees faring on the labour market in Europe? - EU Law and Publications", No. 1/2016, European Commission, Brussels, http://dx.doi.org/10.2767/350756. [1]

EU-FRA (2016), *Thematic focus: Children | European Union Agency for Fundamental Rights*, European Union Agency for Fundamental Rights, http://fra.europa.eu/en/theme/asylum-migration-borders/overviews/focus-children (accessed on 06 September 2018). [47]

European Commission (2017), "On a More Effective Return Policy in the European Union - A Renewed Action Plan", *Communication from the Commission to the European Parliament and the Council*, No. COM(2017) 200 final, European Commission, Brussels, https://ec.europa.eu/home-affairs/sites/homeaffairs/files/what-we-do/policies/european-agenda-migration/20170302_a_more_effective_return_policy_in_the_european_union_-_a_renewed_action_plan_en.pdf (accessed on 17 September 2018). [80]

European Commission (2013), *Study on educational support for newly arrived migrant children: Final Report*, Publications Office of the European Union, Luxembourg, http://dx.doi.org/10.2766/41204.. [23]

Galera, G. et al. (2018), "Integration of Migrants, Refugees and Asylum Seekers in Remote Areas with Declining Populations", *OECD Local Economic and Employment Development (LEED) Working Papers*, No. 2018/03, OECD Publishing, Paris, https://dx.doi.org/10.1787/84043b2a-en. [32]

Galera, G., L. Giannetto and A. Noya (2018), "The Role of Non-state Actors in the Integration of Refugees and Asylum Seekers", *OECD Local Economic and Employment Development (LEED) Working Papers*, No. 2018/02, OECD Publishing, Paris, https://dx.doi.org/10.1787/434c3303-en. [70]

Green, D. et al. (2016), "Immigration, Business Ownership and Employment in Canada", *Analytical Studies Branch Research Paper Series*, No. 375 , Statistics Canada, Ottawa. [61]

Hainmueller, J., D. Hangartner and D. Lawrence (2016), "When lives are put on hold: Lengthy asylum processes decrease employment among refugees", *Science Advances*, Vol. 2/8, pp. e1600432-e1600432, http://dx.doi.org/10.1126/sciadv.1600432. [33]

Health Organization Regional Office for Europe, W. (2016), *Toolkit for assessing health system capacity to manage large influxes of refugees, asylum-seekers and migrants With the support of*, WHO Regional Office for Europe, Copenhagen, http://www.euro.who.int/pubrequest (accessed on 31 August 2018). [42]

Hiebert, D. (2009), "The Economic Integration of Immigrants in Metropolitan Vancouver", *IRPP Choices*, Vol. 15/7, http://irpp.org/wp-content/uploads/assets/research/diversity-immigration-and-integration/the-economic-integration-of-immigrants-in-metropolitan-vancouver/vol15no7.pdf (accessed on 09 September 2018). [65]

ICMC (2011), *Paving the Way: A Handbook on the Reception and Integration of Resettled Refugees*, http://www.refworld.org/docid/543f83494.html (accessed on 17 September 2018). [73]

IOM (2018), *Assisted Voluntary Return and Reintegration 2017 - Key Highlights*. [79]

IOM (2015), *Enhancing the Safety and Sustainability of the Return and Reintegration of Victims of Trafficking*, International Organization for Migration, Paris, https://publications.iom.int/system/files/pdf/essrrvt_en_0.pdf (accessed on 18 September 2018). [83]

Jenkinson, R. et al. (2016), *Settlement experiences of recently arrived humanitarian migrants*, Australian Institute of Family Studies, https://aifs.gov.au/sites/default/files/publication-documents/bnla-fs1-settlement-experiences.pdf (accessed on 15 February 2018). [5]

Klaver, J. and I. van der Welle (2009), *VluchtelingenWerk Integratiebarometer 2009 en onderzoek naar de integratie van vluchtelingen in Nederland.*, VluchtelingenWerk Nederland, Rotterdam, https://www.regioplan.nl/publicaties/rapporten/vluchtelingenwerk_integratiebarometer_2009_een_onderzoek_naar_de_integratie_van_vluchtelingen_in_nederland (accessed on 17 September 2018). [74]

Blossfeld, H. et al. (eds.) (2017), *Effectiveness of Dutch targeted preschool education policy for disadvantaged children: Evidence from the pre-COOL study*, Edward Elgar, http://dx.doi.org/10.4337/9781786432094. [28]

Liebig, T. and K. Tronstad (2018), "Triple Disadvantage? : A first overview of the integration of refugee women", *OECD Social, Employment and Migration Working Papers*, No. 216, OECD Publishing, Paris, http://dx.doi.org/10.1787/3f3a9612-en. [51]

Matthews, J. (2008), "Schooling and settlement: refugee education in Australia", *International Studies in Sociology of Education*, Vol. 18/1, pp. 31-45, http://dx.doi.org/10.1080/09620210802195947. [19]

McBrien, J. (2005), *Educational Needs and Barriers for Refugee Students in the United States: A Review of the Literature*, American Educational Research Association, http://dx.doi.org/10.2307/3515985. [21]

Médecins Sans Frontières (2017), *Confronting the mental health emergency on Samos and Lesvos*, Médecins Sans Frontières, Athens, https://www.msf.org/sites/msf.org/files/2018-06/confronting-the-mental-health-emergency-on-samos-and-lesvos.pdf (accessed on 31 August 2018). [41]

Mental Health Commission of Canada (2016), *Supporting the Mental Health of Refugees to Canada*, Mental Health Commission of Canada, Ottawa, https://ontario.cmha.ca/wp-content/files/2016/02/Refugee-Mental-Health-backgrounder.pdf (accessed on 07 September 2018). [43]

Nilsson, J. and N. Bunar (2016), "Educational Responses to Newly Arrived Students in Sweden: Understanding the Structure and Influence of Post-Migration Ecology", *Scandinavian Journal of Educational Research*, Vol. 60/4, pp. 399-416, http://dx.doi.org/10.1080/00313831.2015.1024160. [26]

OECD (2018), "Entrepreneurship as a Pathway for Integration for Refugees and Vulnerable Migrants", No. CFE/LEED(2018)24, OECD, Paris. [62]

OECD (2018), "How resilient were OECD health care systems during the "refugee crisis"?", *Migration Policy Debates* 17. [39]

OECD (2018), *Skills on the Move: Migrants in the Survey of Adult Skills*, OECD Skills Studies, OECD Publishing, Paris, http://dx.doi.org/10.1787/9789264307353-en. [10]

OECD (2018), *The Resilience of Students with an Immigrant Background: Factors that Shape Well-being*, OECD Reviews of Migrant Education, OECD Publishing, Paris, http://dx.doi.org/10.1787/9789264292093-en. [17]

OECD (2018), *Working Together for Local Integration of Migrants and Refugees*, OECD Publishing, Paris, http://dx.doi.org/10.1787/9789264085350-en. [56]

OECD (2018), *Working Together: Skills and Labour Market Integration of Immigrants and their Children in Finland*, OECD Publishing, Paris, http://dx.doi.org/10.1787/9789264305250-en. [58]

OECD (2017), *Addressing Forced Displacement through Development Planning and Co-operation: Guidance for Donor Policy Makers and Practitioners*, OECD Development Policy Tools, OECD Publishing, Paris, http://dx.doi.org/10.1787/9789264285590-en. [76]

OECD (2017), *Assessing the contribution of refugees to the development of their host countries*, OECD, Paris, http://www.oecd.org/officialdocuments/publicdisplaydocumentpdf/?cote=DEV/DOC(2017)1&docLanguage=En (accessed on 16 November 2018). [77]

OECD (2017), *Catching Up? Intergenerational Mobility and Children of Immigrants*, OECD Publishing, Paris, http://dx.doi.org/10.1787/9789264288041-en. [52]

OECD (2017), *Entrepreneurship at a Glance 2017*, OECD Publishing, Paris, http://dx.doi.org/10.1787/entrepreneur_aag-2017-en. [60]

OECD (2017), *Finding the way: A discussion of the Finnish migrant integration system*, OECD, Paris, http://www.oecd.org/migration/mig/Finding-the-Way-Finland.pdf (accessed on 06 September 2018). [59]

OECD (2017), *Finding their Way: Labour market integration of refugees in Germany*, OECD Publishing. [7]

OECD (2017), *How does having immigrant parents affect the outcomes of children in Europe? Migration Policy Debates n°14*, OECD Publishing, Paris, http://www.oecd.org/els/mig/How-does-having-immigrant-parents-affect-the-outcomes-of-children-in-Europe.pdf (accessed on 06 September 2018). [54]

OECD (2017), *How's Life? 2017: Measuring Well-being*, OECD Publishing, Paris, https://dx.doi.org/10.1787/how_life-2017-en. [2]

OECD (2017), *International Migration Outlook 2017*, OECD Publishing, Paris, http://dx.doi.org/10.1787/migr_outlook-2017-en. [69]

OECD (2017), *Making Integration Work: Assessment and Recognition of Foreign Qualifications*, Making Integration Work, OECD Publishing, Paris, http://dx.doi.org/10.1787/9789264278271-en. [45]

OECD (2017), *Making Integration Work: Family Migrants*, Making Integration Work, OECD Publishing, Paris, http://dx.doi.org/10.1787/9789264279520-en. [53]

OECD (2017), *Starting Strong V: Transitions from Early Childhood Education and Care to Primary Education*, Starting Strong, OECD Publishing, Paris, http://dx.doi.org/10.1787/9789264276253-en. [29]

OECD (2017), *Who bears the cost of integrating refugees? Migration Policy Debate n°13*, OECD, Paris, https://www.oecd.org/els/mig/migration-policy-debates-13.pdf (accessed on 06 September 2018). [57]

OECD (2016), *International Migration Outlook 2016*, OECD Publishing, Paris, http://dx.doi.org/10.1787/migr_outlook-2016-en. [37]

OECD (2016), *Making Integration Work: Refugees and others in need of protection*, Making Integration Work, OECD Publishing, Paris, http://dx.doi.org/10.1787/9789264251236-en. [31]

OECD (2016), *Working Together: Skills and Labour Market Integration of Immigrants and their Children in Sweden*, OECD Publishing, Paris, https://dx.doi.org/10.1787/9789264257382-en. [48]

OECD (2014), "Labour market integration of immigrants and their children: Developing, activating and using skills", in *International Migration Outlook 2014*, OECD Publishing, Paris, http://dx.doi.org/10.1787/migr_outlook-2014-5-en. [12]

OECD (2008), *Jobs for Immigrants (Vol. 2): Labour Market Integration in Belgium, France, the Netherlands and Portugal*, OECD Publishing, Paris, https://dx.doi.org/10.1787/9789264055605-en. [55]

OECD (2008), "Return Migration: A New Perspective", in *International Migration Outlook 2008*, OECD Publishing, Paris, http://dx.doi.org/10.1787/migr_outlook-2008-7-en. [82]

OECD (2007), *Jobs for Immigrants (Vol. 1): Labour Market Integration in Australia, Denmark, Germany and Sweden*, OECD Publishing, Paris, http://dx.doi.org/10.1787/9789264033603-en. [71]

OECD (2007), "Matching Educational Background and Employment: A Challenge for Immigrants In Host Countries", in *International Migration Outlook 2007*, OECD Publishing, Paris, http://dx.doi.org/10.1787/migr_outlook-2007-4-en. [14]

OECD (2006), *International Migration Outlook 2006*, OECD Publishing, Paris, http://dx.doi.org/10.1787/migr_outlook-2006-en. [50]

OECD/EU (2018), *Indicators of Immigrant Integration 2018: Settling In*, OECD Publishing. [3]

OECD/EU (2015), *Indicators of Immigrant Integration 2015: Settling In*, OECD Publishing, Paris, http://dx.doi.org/10.1787/9789264234024-en. [13]

OECD/The European Commission (2013), *The Missing Entrepreneurs: Policies for Inclusive Entrepreneurship in Europe*, OECD Publishing, Paris, http://dx.doi.org/10.1787/9789264188167-en. [63]

Picot, G. and A. Sweetman (2011), "Canadian Immigration Policy and Immigrant Economic Outcomes: Why the Differences in Outcomes between Sweden and Canada?", *IZA Policy Papers*, https://ideas.repec.org/p/iza/izapps/pp25.html (accessed on 18 September 2018). [15]

Rath, J. et al. (2011), *Promoting ethnic entrepreneurship in European cities*, European Union, Luxembourg, https://www.coe.int/t/democracy/migration/Source/migration/congress_public_3.pdf (accessed on 09 September 2018). [64]

Rezaei, S., M. Goli and S. Møballe (2006), *"Indvandreres tætte netværk: Katalysator eller hæmsko for innovation og vækst? – Et studie af formelle og uformelle netværksrelationers betydning for dynamikken i indvandrerejede virksomheder".: Hovedrapport & Policyanbefalinger*, https://forskning.ruc.dk/da/publications/indvandreres-t%C3%A6tte-netv%C3%A6rk-katalysator-eller-h%C3%A6msko-for-innovatio (accessed on 07 September 2018). [66]

Salvi del Pero, A. et al. (2016), "Policies to promote access to good-quality affordable housing in OECD countries", *OECD Social, Employment and Migration Working Papers*, No. 176, OECD Publishing, Paris, http://dx.doi.org/10.1787/5jm3p5gl4djd-en. [35]

Scanlon, K., M. Fernández Arrigoitia and C. Whitehead (2015), "Social housing in Europe. European Policy Analysis", *European Policy Analysis*, Vol. 17, pp. 1-12, http://www.sieps.se (accessed on 04 September 2018). [38]

Sirin, S. and L. Rogers-Sirin (2015), *The educational and mental health needs of Syrian refugee children*, https://www.migrationpolicy.org/sites/default/files/publications/FCD-Sirin-Rogers-FINAL.pdf (accessed on 09 September 2018). [24]

SNIS (2015), *The children of refugees in Europe: aspirations, social and economic lives, identity and transnational linkages - Country reports*, Swiss Network for International Studies, Geneva, http://www.academia.edu/34705288/The_children_of_refugees_in_Europe_aspirations_social_and_economic_lives_identity_and_transnational_linkages_-_Country_reports (accessed on 03 September 2018). [22]

Suárez-Orozco, C. et al. (2011), "Growing Up in the Shadows: The Developmental Implications of Unauthorized Status", *Harvard Educational Review*, Vol. 81/3, pp. 438-473, http://dx.doi.org/10.17763/haer.81.3.g23x203763783m75. [25]

UNHCR (2018), *Global Trends: Forced Displacement in 2017*, http://www.unhcr.org/5b27be547.pdf (accessed on 30 August 2018). [75]

UNHCR (2017), *Assets of Refugees in Zaatari camp: A Profile of Skills*, UNHCR, http://www.unhcr.orghttp://data.unhcr.org/syrianrefugees/regional.php-www.facebook.com/UNHCRJordan-twitter.com/ (accessed on 16 November 2018). [78]

UNHCR (2017), *Assets of Refugees in Zataari camp: A Profile of Skills*, UNHCR. [9]

UNICEF (2017), *A child is a child: Protecting children on the move from violence, abuse and exploitation*, http://www.unicef.org/publications/index_95956.html. [46]

WHO Regional Committee for Europe (2016), *Strategy and action plan for refugee and migrant health in the WHO European Region*, WHO Regional Office for Europe, Copenhagen, http://www.euro.who.int/__data/assets/pdf_file/0004/314725/66wd08e_MigrantHealthStrategyActionPlan_160424.pdf?ua=1 (accessed on 31 August 2018). [44]

Wilkinson, L. (2002), "Factors Influencing the Academic Success of Refugee Youth in Canada", *Journal of Youth Studies*, Vol. 5/2, pp. 173-193, http://dx.doi.org/10.1080/13676260220134430. [20]

World Bank (2018), *Asylum Seekers in the European Union: Building Evidence to Inform Policy Making*, World Bank, Washington, http://documents.worldbank.org/curated/en/832501530296269142/pdf/127818-V1-WP-P160648-PUBLIC-Disclosed-7-2-2018.pdf (accessed on 14 November 2018). [8]

Chapter 3. Anticipating, monitoring and reacting to inflows of refugees and other vulnerable migrants

Shortcomings in collection, circulation and use of information hinder public policy action in dealing with inflows of refugees and other vulnerable migrants and supporting their integration outcomes. This chapter examines how systems can better anticipate demand and how outcomes can be monitored over time.

Can early warning mechanisms help prevent a crisis in the face of future large-scale inflows?

The world was caught largely off guard by the mass migration movements from the Middle East and Africa in 2015-16, even if there were ample early warning signs (OECD, 2018[1]). Similarly, increases in asylum seeking in other regions of the world have often occurred following early warning signs that were not adequately captured. Putting together an early warning system requires investment and collaboration. A number of considerations can be taken into account in developing a platform (OECD, 2018[1]).

First, early warning and alert systems based on monitoring flows in real time require significant resources and information sharing among countries, as well as updated intelligence on the functioning and the evolution of smuggling networks.

Second, early warning systems require a good understanding of trigger points to minimise the risks of ignoring relevant signals (false negatives) and of overstating irrelevant signals (false positives).

By linking to specific analysis of diasporas and social networks, early warning and alert systems may pick up the scope of looming migration surges and their destinations.

New data allow for expanding the range of signals to consider. "Big data" – high-volume, velocity and variety data – have allowed fresh analysis to be used in developing early warning systems. Communication-based information sources such as social media, Internet searches, smartphone apps, the IP addresses of website logins and emails, and call detail records all represent grist for analysis. Geolocation further increases the potential of these methods, but also the risks connected with privacy and confidentiality (Box 3.1).

Box 3.1. Big data use in early warning systems to detect risk of forced migration

Two examples of using big data to provide early warning are the Gdelt project and Google Analytics. Gdelt identifies global trends and emerging social, political and economic risks worldwide. Monitoring news in over 100 languages, Gdelt can track events, locations, organisations, people, etc. Google Analytics' search term frequency reveals terms that have been searched in great numbers, as well as the language in and location from which they were searched. (Böhme, Gröger and Stöhr, 2017[2]; Connor, 2017[3]) have determined that under certain conditions, search query data can allow forecasts of migration flows.

Source: (OECD, 2018[1]).

Foresight methods focused on specific migration categories or corridors may inform policy if the time horizon is not too distant (less than 10-15 years). Longer time horizons may limit their relevance for policy makers. However, these longer-range exercises can help build consensus around long-term challenges and objectives, and help future-proof policies.

Due to data limitations and uncertainties, tools to model flows of forced migration are resource-intensive and relatively fragile, notably in the context of major external shocks. Nevertheless, in cases where the investment can be mutualised and the results are fully integrated into a multi-dimensional/inter-ministerial response system, it may well be worth investing in such tools.

More could be done to strengthen co-ordination efforts with regard to the way data are gathered for forecasting and the sharing of data within and beyond the European Union, with transit countries and with other OECD countries.

Whatever information system is adopted, policy makers must trust that information so that they act promptly upon it with a full understanding of the uncertainties – because foresight will indeed contain uncertainties.

A "post mortem" exercise should also be undertaken systematically following all major crises and shocks at national and regional levels, in order to improve policy response and preparedness. One recent key lesson is that although information systems were in place prior to 2015/2016, policy makers did not always act on the indications it provided.

What information needs to be improved to better monitor integration outcomes and inform integration policy?

While information on flows and stocks has steadily improved, much remains to be done to improve monitoring of the integration outcomes of refugees and other vulnerable migrants, and linking of this monitoring to the evaluation and development of integration policy. A recent international statistics forum held at the OECD pointed to shortcomings in statistics on refugees and other migrants in vulnerable situations (Box 3.2).

The measurement of well-being outcomes by migrant status – through for example identifying refugees separately from other categories of migrants – is very challenging for those gathering official statistics. While administrative data sources often include information on migration status, household surveys are the most appropriate vehicle for measuring well-being outcomes across a range of dimensions – but then, household surveys rarely identify migrants by category of entry. Further, sample design that is appropriate for the overall population may not be sufficient to capture information about migrant groups. Since migrants both tend to account for a relatively small share of the population in OECD countries and tend to live in geographically segregated areas of the country, sample sizes may be too small.

Censuses or administrative records that contain the most detailed information on migrants in terms of provenance, reason for migrating and key demographic variables only rarely include information on integration outcomes beyond income, labour market status and education. Some OECD countries, such as Australia and Canada, are making use of integrated data sets that link administrative data with censuses or other surveys.

The need for more detailed and granular data on migrant outcomes than what is found in surveys requires a sufficiently large sample and the inclusion of additional questions to identify different sub-groups. Adapting the methodology of existing surveys, such as by boosting sample sizes, will improve the representativeness of the migrant sample obtained (Šteinbuka, 2009[4]).

Improving survey design to reduce non-response rates will also need to be considered. The European Union Labour Force Survey (EU LFS) and the European Union Statistics on Income and Living Conditions (EU SILC) have both included special ad hoc modules on migrants' outcomes in recent years; these experiences can inform improvements to the measurement of migrant outcomes in other surveys and countries.

Meeting the need for more detailed and granular data on migrant outcomes will also require inclusion of additional survey questions that allow identifying different sub-groups. In addition to the important demographic and socio-economic variables that are usually included in household surveys (e.g. age, gender, educational attainment), some migrant-specific questions should be considered. These include country of birth, duration of stay and reasons for migrating. The experiences of countries that are already using such variables – for example, from 2017 the German Labour Force Survey will include a question on reasons for migrating – could provide useful lessons for others.

In cases where it would be too difficult to modify the methodology of an existing survey, and where resources allow, developing a special, targeted survey of migrant outcomes could be considered.

Special efforts are needed to ensure that data collections cover and enable identification of the most vulnerable migrants, especially those who are unlikely to be reached through standard household surveys. Some countries have made advances in targeting specific migrant groups who may be at greater risk of well-being deprivations; this is the case with Australia's Building a New Life in Australia survey, which focuses on the experiences of recently arrived humanitarian migrants.

More longitudinal data are needed to understand the evolution of different well-being outcomes for individual migrants over time. More national longitudinal surveys of migrant outcomes should be carried out where possible, and efforts to harmonise surveys across countries could help to facilitate international comparisons.

Box 3.2. The International Forum on Migration Statistics

To address the gaps in knowledge and statistics regarding migration, the first-ever International Forum on Migration Statistics was held on 15-16 January 2018 at the OECD (www.oecd.org/migration/forum-migration-statistics). Much of the discussion at the forum focused on refugees and migrants in vulnerable situations. Over 500 people from almost all countries of the OECD and many non-members participated in this event, which featured 240 speakers and presenters. Some of the high-level keynote speakers were from partner organisations (IOM and the UN) and from national statistical offices (NSOs. Conclusions were published by the OECD in a joint brief with the International Organization for Migration and the United Nations Department of Economic and Social Affairs (2018[5]).

In addition, a Call to Action – "Protecting children on the move starts with better data" – was jointly published in February 2018 by UNICEF, UNHCR, IOM, Eurostat and the OECD (2018[6]). The publication was prompted by the observation that data are not collected, or are too poor, to provide information about children on the move: their age and gender; where they come from; where they are going; whether they move with their families or alone; how they fare along the way; and what their vulnerabilities are. These important gaps in child-specific information need to be addressed.

References

Böhme, M., A. Gröger and T. Stöhr (2017), *Searching for a Better Life: Now-casting International Migration with Online Search Keywords*, https://www.wider.unu.edu/sites/default/files/STOEHR%2C%20Tobias_paper.pdf (accessed on 06 September 2018). [2]

Connor, P. (2017), *Can Google Trends Forecast Forced Migration Flows? Perhaps, but Under Certain Conditions*, Pew Research Center, Washington. [3]

IOM/OECD/UN DESA (2018), *What were the key messages of the International Forum on Migration Statistics*, OECD Publishing. [5]

OECD (2018), *Can we anticipate future migration flows? Migration Policy Debate n°16*, OECD, Paris, http://www.oecd.org/migration/mig/migration-policy-debate-16.pdf (accessed on 06 September 2018). [1]

Šteinbuka, I. (2009), *How to improve social surveys to provide better statistics on migrants*, http://ec.europa.eu/eurostat/documents/1001617/4339944/Improving-survey-data1-Steinbuka.pdf/e90f6527-af4d-4585-8f3d-d7dde093b148 (accessed on 15 February 2018). [4]

UNICEF et al. (2018), *A call to action: Protecting children on the move starts with better data*. [6]

Chapter 4. Policy approaches for the integration of refugees and other vulnerable migrants

This chapter provides a series of recommendations for ensuring better integration of refugees and other vulnerable migrants. It summarises recommendations in areas ranging from initial arrival, social integration, institutional support and co-ordination among actors, and international co-operation.

This report aims to help OECD countries be better prepared to ensure integration of refugees and other vulnerable migrants, notably in the context of sudden and large inflows. Building on the recommendations of the Global Compact on Refugees [as well as on previous OECD work (OECD, 2016[1]), and drawing on the recent experience of OECD countries synthesised in these pages, the report identifies a number of policies that can support the fair and effective integration of refugees and other vulnerable migrants.

The study has discussed a number of different target groups, each with different needs. The following summary may serve as a policy toolkit to be drawn on by countries, according to national circumstances and in line with domestic legislation. Five main areas for concrete action are identified.

Smoothing the transition from reception to integration

The immediate needs of vulnerable migrants and people seeking international protection are covered at reception by providing temporary shelter and subsistence, as well as emergency health services. For school-age children, continuity of education is also essential. However, asylum seekers and vulnerable migrants who have a high probability of remaining need to start the integration process as quickly as possible. The following actions can support this transition:

- Implement fair and fast processes for identifying the vulnerabilities of recently arrived migrants to assist decision making on asylum claims.

- Adapt reception and integration support services to the specific needs of each migrant in a situation of vulnerability, with special attention to migrant children and women.

- Ensure that integration services, including language training, are available as soon as possible for those with a high probability of remaining. Rapid access to economic opportunities for this group will give labour market integration a head start.

- Work with local receiving communities, if possible before arrival, to address their needs as well as potential concerns regarding the reception and integration of incoming vulnerable migrants.

- Develop contingency planning or emergency response plans at national and regional levels for all stakeholders involved in the reception and integration of refugees and other vulnerable migrants in case of mass inflow. Co-ordination mechanisms should be in place that can be rapidly activated.

Improving short- and longer-term employability and access to social services

Support to refugees and other vulnerable migrants that will improve their employability can help them realise their full economic potential. This is of utmost importance in terms of economic impact for the host country, but also for acceptance and social inclusion in the local community. The following actions can help economic and social integration:

- Profile, recognise, develop and apply their skills – bringing to bear formal and non-formal qualifications – including through skills recognition systems, access to general education, flexible vocational training, and employment counselling.

- Promote early access to language training, adapted to the skill profile of beneficiaries and tailored to the development of occupation-specific language skills.

- Facilitate access to public employment services and employment promotion schemes such as wage subsidies and other incentives, public work schemes, internships and access to temporary work agencies, as appropriate.

- Identify and address obstacles to geographic mobility, to ensure that refugees and other vulnerable migrants are not prevented from moving to take up better employment opportunities within the country.

- Support initiatives to advance social inclusion, including through integration courses focused on host society values as well as migrants' rights and duties.

- Facilitate the introduction of unaccompanied minors and other vulnerable migrant children in both the school system and in apprenticeships by providing individual support and adequate transition support, notably to equip them with language and other requisite skills.

- Improve the resilience of health and education systems to large inflows of vulnerable migrants, and better exploit the potential of technology and innovative approaches to deliver health care and training, notably in less populated areas.

Promoting economic and social acceptance

While labour market integration and economic self-reliance enable social integration, they do not guarantee it. More action is needed to make sure that refugees and other vulnerable migrants find their way in the host society. Areas of action can include the following:

- Ensure that employers and employers' associations are involved in facilitating integration of refugees and other vulnerable migrants in the workplace through partnerships involving private sector and local authorities.

- Remove institutional obstacles to entrepreneurship for refugees and offer packages of support to those with entrepreneurial potential – including coaching and mentoring – to help them create their own jobs and build professional and social networks.

- Support social partners and civil society – including local communities, charitable groups and diasporas – in integration efforts, to foster a sense of belonging.

- Support equal working conditions between national and migrant workers by implementing fair recruitment practices and minimum wage coverage, by formalising informal work for those having a legal right to work, and through providing access to remedies against discrimination and exploitation.

- Develop sound communication strategies to inform the public about the integration process of refugees and other vulnerable migrants, so as to increase awareness of the challenges they encounter and of the benefits of successful labour market integration.

- Use websites, social media and other means of communication to inform refugees and other vulnerable migrants about opportunities, rights and obligations related to social and labour market integration in host countries and reintegration in origin countries.

Supporting sub-national authorities

Granting the fundamental role of national integration policies and the impetus often provided by government-led strategies, sub-national authorities often play a significant role in implementing important components of national policies, and may also provide key integration services through their own policies. It is therefore important to ensure proper support for their actions and appropriate co-ordination among different levels of government. Support can be provided through these actions:

- Ensure that dialogue on integration policies is held with local and regional authorities and among sub-national governance levels.

- Encourage local authorities to reach out to refugees and other vulnerable migrants and ensure equal access to local public services and opportunities for instance by providing early guidance, setting up one-stop-shops with civic and administrative information available in several languages.

- Provide the incentive for effective co-ordination among public and non-state actors at the appropriate scale for refugee integration, and define standards and norms in service delivery.

- Elaborate and implement dispersal policies in concert with local authorities, taking into account housing capacity, the local labour market situation, and available access to integration and social services.

- Ensure that funding is commensurate with the distribution of competencies and the relative caseload at different government levels and across regions.

Increasing international co-operation on crisis management and integration

Continuity of services through the migration journey, as well as co-ordination of the different actors at national, regional and international levels, is central to effective integration systems. Co-operation should be developed in the following areas:

- Co-ordinate among countries of first asylum, transit countries and host countries to speed up processes and better target services to different categories of vulnerability. Find means to transmit information, for example regarding health situations and educational attainment, collected by states and their agencies at different stages of the journey. Ensure that this information is shared in the context of resettlement or relocation.

- Co-ordinate among host countries to develop appropriate early warning systems and to share good practices and responsibility, as no country alone can address large and sudden inflows of refugees and other vulnerable migrants. Take this international dimension into account in national contingency planning and emergency response plans.

- Address long- and short-term needs with inputs on humanitarian-development-peace coherence, in order to better identify specific issues that need to be addressed. Develop regional multi-stakeholder response plans to improve coherence in humanitarian assistance and development approaches to forced displacement.

- Find the right types of financing to address crisis, fragility and forced displacement situations. Extend progress at the global and regional level to the national level.

References

OECD (2016), *Making Integration Work: Refugees and others in need of protection*, Making Integration Work, OECD Publishing, Paris, http://dx.doi.org/10.1787/9789264251236-en. [1]

ORGANISATION FOR ECONOMIC CO-OPERATION AND DEVELOPMENT

The OECD is a unique forum where governments work together to address the economic, social and environmental challenges of globalisation. The OECD is also at the forefront of efforts to understand and to help governments respond to new developments and concerns, such as corporate governance, the information economy and the challenges of an ageing population. The Organisation provides a setting where governments can compare policy experiences, seek answers to common problems, identify good practice and work to co-ordinate domestic and international policies.

The OECD member countries are: Australia, Austria, Belgium, Canada, Chile, the Czech Republic, Denmark, Estonia, Finland, France, Germany, Greece, Hungary, Iceland, Ireland, Israel, Italy, Japan, Korea, Latvia, Lithuania, Luxembourg, Mexico, the Netherlands, New Zealand, Norway, Poland, Portugal, the Slovak Republic, Slovenia, Spain, Sweden, Switzerland, Turkey, the United Kingdom and the United States. The European Union takes part in the work of the OECD.

OECD Publishing disseminates widely the results of the Organisation's statistics gathering and research on economic, social and environmental issues, as well as the conventions, guidelines and standards agreed by its members.

www.ingramcontent.com/pod-product-compliance
Lightning Source LLC
LaVergne TN
LVHW061943070526
838199LV00060B/3952